# PROFESSOR DR. P. HENNIPMAN
# LECTURES IN ECONOMICS
## Theory, Institutions, Policy

VOLUME 5

NORTH-HOLLAND
AMSTERDAM · NEW YORK · OXFORD

# AMONG ECONOMISTS
## Reflections of a Neo-Classical Post Keynesian

JAN PEN

*Professor of Economics, University of Groningen*

*Translation:*

TREVOR S. PRESTON

1985

NORTH-HOLLAND
AMSTERDAM · NEW YORK · OXFORD

ISBN 0-444-87636-7


*Publishers:*
ELSEVIER SCIENCE PUBLISHERS B.V.
P.O. Box 1991
1000 BZ  Amsterdam
The Netherlands

*Sole distributors for the U.S.A. and Canada:*
ELSEVIER SCIENCE PUBLISHING COMPANY INC.
52 Vanderbilt Avenue
New York, N.Y. 10017
U.S.A.


PRINTED IN THE NETHERLANDS

*The 'Professor Dr. P. Hennipman Stichting' was founded at the initiative of the 'Kring van Amsterdamse Economen' (Circle of Amsterdam Economists) on the occasion of Professor Hennipman's retirement from his Chair in the Faculty of Economics at the University of Amsterdam. The Foundation is administered by a Board of Dutch economists who are, for the greater part, university professors.*

*P. Hennipman served the Amsterdam Faculty from 1938 until 1974, covering a broad field of subjects in economic theory in his brilliant and very thorough lectures. In this way, he trained and inspired many generations of students, and equipped them with analytical tools and scientific practices of inestimable value in their careers in science, education, business and politics. Like his lectures, Hennipman's publications are characterized by his almost unique way of carefully and profoundly weighing all aspects of the subject, based on sharp-witted thinking and reasoning, combined with linguistic refinements, on the one hand, and on an encyclopaedic knowledge of relevant literature on the other.*

*In honour of P. Hennipman, the Foundation has undertaken to organize, every two years, a lecture by an outstanding economist, and these lectures will be published in an elaborated form as monographs. Fortunately, it has been possible to co-ordinate this goal with the activities of the Professor F. de Vries Foundation, and as a result, lectures will be published annually under the alternate auspices of the two Foundations in a combined series entitled* 'Lectures in Economics–Theory, Institutions, Policy'.

# FOREWORD

Jan Pen, born in 1921, studied economics at the University of Amsterdam. He gained his doctor's degree under Professor Hennipman. From 1947 to 1956 he worked at the Ministry of Economic Affairs. Since 1956 he is Professor of Economics at the University of Groningen. He was nominated a Fellow of the Royal Academy of Sciences in 1972. He received an Honorary Degree at the Free University of Brussels in 1974.

The contribution of Jan Pen to economic theory testifies a clear vision and much wit. It is varied too, as is apparent merely from the books which he published in English; *The Wage Rate under Bargaining*, Cambridge, 1959; *Modern Economics*, Harmondsworth, 1965; *Harmony and Conflict in Modern Society*, Maidenhead, 1965; *A Primer in International Trade*, New York, 1967; *Income Distribution*, London, 1971.

Jan Pen delivered the fourth Hennipman Lecture on April 4, 1984. The Hennipman Foundation is happy to include in the series 'Lectures in Economics' this monograph on methodological questions which is a substantially elaborated version of the lecture.

J.J. Klant

# CONTENTS

# Contents

Chapter I

# A QUARRELSOME LOT?

Most economists have regular jobs that keep them off the streets. They sit in offices and maximize unknown utilities; their own or somebody else's. The utilities are unknown, probably to those who maximize them and certainly to outside observers. One thing we know for certain is that the economists turn inputs into outputs. They transform more or less raw data into cooked data, cooked data into information, and information into knowledge. Sometimes they turn knowledge into wisdom. They supply the results of their efforts to other people, perhaps also economists, who sit in offices too. Some of the users are decision-makers, among them a number of professional economists. The whole process takes place within government agencies, industries, banks, insurance companies, trade unions, international organizations. Some of these economists – they are nearly all men, nothwithstanding the existence of Alice Rivlin – call themselves managers, or executives, or consultants, or research workers, or bookkeepers. Only a few of them have read Jan Kregel's *The Reconstruction of Political Economy* (London, 1973), which is a pity, for this book stimulates the mind, and none has read Piero Sraffa's *Production of Commodities By Means of Commodities* (Cambridge, 1960). They regard themselves as experts: cool, technology-oriented people. They manufacture an intermediate product that for the greater part does not leave the organization.

These employees are part of the corporate culture. Though the corporation is not necessarily a model of radiant harmony, most economists would describe their various activities as essentially peaceful. It is a part of their expertise to find reasonable solutions for conflicting aims, on the basis of the best possible factual information. They determine the restrictions and conditions that limit the possibilities of attaining given objectives. They seek the optimum policy mix. Rationality is their guiding light. If a person were to ask: 'Are you a member of that quarrelsome profession?', the question would encounter a certain surprise: 'Who, me? Aren't you confusing me with somebody else?'

And indeed another subculture of economists does exist. They maximize their utilities by operating in the political arena. They advise politicians, or they are professional politicians themselves. They also belong to the knowledge industry, but they produce a collective good, or bad, according to the consumers' tastes. They voice ideas on public issues, and public issues are controversial issues. This is, of course, particularly true of economic policy, where interests clash. The voices ring loud, though not always clear. They are busily outwitting each other.

These economists mingle with journalists, and some behave like journalists themselves, for they write in magazines and newspapers. They appear on television and comment on government policy. These comments are mainly critical, which is the normal state of affairs in a democracy, though some economists support the government and justify what it is doing. That means that they tend to describe the current situation as rather satisfactory, whereas other observers perceive misery and doom. All this creates an atmosphere of dissent and strife. Economics is a house divided.

Now it might be argued that these political economists are not scientists, but citizens. Citizens disagree in their capacity of farmers, taxpayers, trade unionists, businessmen, socialists, neo-conservatives. Economists defend the interests of these groups, for whatever reason: their parents are farmers, their wives are in business, they are taxpayers or conservatives themselves, or they are paid for their opinions. The argument is perfectly correct. Nevertheless, the distinction between the professional economist and the citizen is beset with difficulties. For economics is what economists do, and some members of the profession proffer their advice subtly disguised as scientific commentary, without overt policy conclusions. The most effective rhetoric leaves its conclusions to the listener. The confusion is confounded by the fact that politicians have an understandable habit of quoting those economists whose ideas are in line with theirs, thereby stressing the fact, disputable as it may be, that their own views are supported by economic theory. In this way even the more or less distant scientists are drawn into the citizens' battle.

This brings us to a third subculture: the academic community of disinterested scholars and teachers. They see themselves as economic scientists or economists in the strict sense. They produce books and articles. The teachers teach what the scholars have thought up. Now here we encounter a contradiction. The scholars are said to disagree. They are divided into schools, combating each other on first principles, models, research results, methodology, relevance, whatever. But the textbooks display a surprising degree of similarity. True, they change over the years – they grow fatter, they contain new chapters (market disequilibrium is a recent addition), more coloured graphs and recently illustrations too; but at a given moment in time the substance of the textbooks is rather homogeneous (1).

This means that all professional economists of a given vintage have been brought up along the same lines. They all know their micro-economics, macro-economics, general equilibrium theory, theory of international trade. There is a large corpus of received doctrine. It has been called the Neo-Classical Neo-Keynesian Synthesis. Economists use a common language, full of supply and demand, elasticities, consumption functions, investment functions, dynamically stable or unstable equilibria, comparative costs. These textbooks are synthetic, or eclectic, or instrumental. They represent a mainstream – so much so that various minorities like Marxists, institutionalists, adherents of the New Right speak disapprovingly of the Dominating Paradigm. Obviously, there is more conformity within the profession than the gloomy diagnosis which says that economists never agree on anything would have it. We have a paradox here, and one of the minor goals of this essay is to solve it.

Now the truth-seeking scholars follow a hybrid vocation

as well. It cannot be denied that many of them do research in a field where a consensus is obvious. Those applying linear algebra, topology and other modern techniques to economic problems are a tranquil lot. Their work is far from the madding crowd. It is also true that an economist may well write about the relation between economic theory and economic policy without losing his detached scientific attitude. The proof of this possibility is furnished by the work of Pieter Hennipman (2), who stresses Weber's dictum that economic theory can never make policy recommendations, but who also says (translation from the Dutch): 'It is nevertheless indisputably so that economics owes its growth to its present position largely to the endeavour to improve economic policy. The questions that arise here have always been a challenge and a wellspring, a touchstone for its capabilities and a mirror held up to its results' (p. 20). Hennipman constantly emphasizes that there is no such thing as a 'correct economic policy', or 'economic objectives'. Science and policy must be sharply segregated, but theory must definitely be relevant to policy, if at all possible. This point of view is endorsed in the following.

But other scientists are sometimes difficult to tell apart from ordinary citizens with outspoken preferences for right and wrong. They consider it part of their calling to explain some kind of Good Society to their contemporaries. The Nobel prize does not serve as a criterion for distinguishing the political from the non-political scholars: Koopmans, Arrow and Debreu do not join in the debate between the citizens, but Tinbergen, Friedman, Meade and Stigler do. The influence of the latter group on political thought and action is considerable, though Stigler himself tends to deny this. The trouble is, of course, that this influence works in rather different directions (3). This suggests that the true source of strife between economists is politics, not economics. If this were the case, our view of the profession would be greatly simplified. Unfortunately, things are not that simple. Surely the economics of Meade and Tinbergen on the one hand and of Friedman and Stigler on the other are different (4).

That this is so is best illustrated by the books that such authors publish on their view of society. These are only rarely genuine political tracts – Milton Friedman's *Free to Choose* (New York, 1980) is an exception. An erudite work like J.E. Meade's *Stagnation, Volume I: Wage Fixing* (London, 1982), despite its academic nature, contains a certain view on the economic *ensemble,* which almost automatically leads to the conclusion that free wage determination fits badly into a society pursuing full employment. This political opinion fits in with a coherent whole. And even Kenneth Arrow's work (*Social Choice and Individual Values,* New York, 1951) has a certain relevance to our view of democratic policy, i.e. to the effectiveness of voting procedures. Theoretical economics almost always has an influence on our view of society's functioning and vice versa. I shall argue below that this is a good thing – a genuine economist combines knowledge of abstract eonomics with a sense of relative values and a feeling for politics. The Good, the True and the Beautiful accompany us at all times. Perhaps economics is in fact a Moral Science? My answer, which I do not want to impose on the reader, is: yes. As a result of this disagreement creeps in and the question is how such moral differences of opinion can be localized and assessed. To what extent can we decide who is right? The very unsatisfactory answer is: in many cases we cannot.

Yet the idea that economists quarrel on every conceivable occasion is a popular misunderstanding. It is the direct result of another misunderstanding, namely that the intention of economics is to give good advice. An economist is someone who tells someone else what to do. This is not so, but the idea is encouraged by many members of the profession and above all by their use of language. The terminology suggests that economists know what is good for people: optimum choice, rational behaviour, maximum satisfaction, efficient allocation, optimum mix of policy instruments. This terminology occurs not only in corporate culture and political culture, but also among the disinterested scholars. That gives the profession a certain prestige, just like that enjoyed by doctors and ministers of religion. Unfortunately, that prestige is shaky. It can easily reverse itself, namely when things are going badly and economists get the blame. The 'economic crisis' is often nothing else but the usual old recession or the usual old depression, with its unemployment, its bankruptcies and its frightening budgetary deficits. The misunderstanding that economists have nothing better to do than give firm recommendations must be contested in any account of the profession, and this essay is no exception to that rule (and still, I hope that you will ask: does the author believe that economics is a Moral Science?)

Incidentally, there is no clear-cut distinction between

laymen and professional economists. For that too is characteristic of the culture of economics: everybody gets in on the act, it's a free-for-all. The experts are distinguished by their academic degree, although that's not certain either: one of the first two Nobel prize winners is not a graduate economist but a physicist; engineers have made a major contribution, especially in France; and on the Continent economists are often by origin lawyers. The laymen distinguish themselves by the fact that they make a number of systematic errors more frequently; for instance, they often believe that the vigorous pronouncement of a value judgment is enough to attain the desired goal, and economists are somewhat more cautious. Laymen also fall victim in many cases to the Fallacy of Composition – but professional economists too can make systematic mistakes, and I am not so sure that the rational expectations school is free from this particular fallacy. Personally I am not in favour of a clear-cut demarcation between professional and non-professional economists. I prefer a distinction between correct and incorrect statements.

This essay is mainly concerned with the question of what the mix is between agreement and disagreement in economics. I have the feeling that many disputes between economists are comparable to arguments between lawyers in a court case. These jurists defend opposite positions, but nobody will derive a fission in legal logic from their opposed pleadings. Their arguments – full of metaphors, rhetoric, references to accepted principles – are submitted to a judge who has to decide who is right and who is wrong.

Of course, that's what we need in science: a judge whose

authority is accepted by all parties. The difficulty is that such an authority does not exist. Justice can be *done* – perhaps because it's so slippery. But truth has to be evident. Economics does in fact have its unshakable certainties, or something near enough to be regarded as unshakable. However, there are no real authorities. And even some certainties prove to be the subject of permanent debate. Now it tends to be a rhetorical custom to make an occasional appeal to some author or the other – 'Joan Robinson has proved that a heterogeneous stock of capital goods can be expressed numerically only by capitalizing the expected returns' – but such an appeal is a debater's artifice. The opposite party can point out that Joan Robinson has made mistakes before, just like Keynes himself, come to that, and that every business economist manages to value heterogeneous machines in terms of money and put them on the balance sheet. Appealing to authorities is often a sign of an unscientific mentality – Marxists do it, and that's a bad omen.

Efforts have been made (by Thomas Kuhn and others) to obviate this difficulty by assuming that there is such a thing as a scientific forum or an invisible college. These are thus the qualified scholars in a given professional field. If they agree on something, we have found the truth, be it provisionally. The idea is optimistic and inspired the foundation of the British Royal Society (originally called the invisible college). The difficulty is that these professional colleagues do not always agree with one another – and that is exactly the suspicion that falls on economists. An additional problem is that consensus does not necessarily beget

the truth. There are collective misunderstandings that endure for a long time. For instance, the invisible college of
economists maintained for generations that general over-
production was impossible; underspending would be excluded by the price mechanism, scarcity, Say's Law or
whatever you want to call it. A healthy distrust of received
opinions is to the critical scientist's credit. At least one
trend-setting economist has acquired a certain fame by taking this distrust so far that he practically identifies Conventional Wisdom with collective stupidity.

But if we embrace the latter hypercritical view, we easily
enter a state of general scepticism, in which every statement
is left hanging in the air and we have to rely solely on our
own logic. That makes too great a demand of our talent
for improvisation. It is not efficient. After all, we've learnt
all kinds of things and taken them for granted, and we have
to use them too – otherwise life becomes extremely primi-
tive. We believe in the multiplication tables and in the
proposition that a permanent budgetary deficit amounting
to a given fraction of national income $z$, at a given and constant growth rate $y$ of national income, leads in the long
run to a ratio between national debt and national income
equal to $z/y$. That is unassailable. Propositions exist that
have to be upheld, on pain of the verdict: 'that person's not
right in the head'. Anyone who claims that two plus two
is five is a joker, an interrogator out of Orwell's *Nineteen
Eighty-four*, or should have his head examined. (Or he ad-
heres to a deep philosophy which, however, is not recognized in the grocery store. Economics is a grocery store.)

The latter is perhaps not a bad definition of truth. Truth

is what has to be endorsed by somebody who's right in the head. In economics truth is what has to be endorsed by a professional economist who's right in the head. I think that the body of statements that are covered by this definition in economics can boast a very considerable size. And that includes the authoritative nature of much that we have learnt, but also of what we have always known.

However, there are also statements, inside and outside economics, to which the criterion of truth hardly relates, if at all. In fact we see a whole scale. If somebody says: 'there are fifty people in this hall', it can be investigated whether that is correct. There may be doubt as to whether a certain object must be regarded as a person, or whether some have to be counted as two; there may be someone in a cupboard or sitting under a table – but a certain degree of agreement can be reached. Anyone who mentions a number that is very wide of the truth has made a wrong estimate and will, after some debate, certainly realize that. But if someone asserts: 'it would be much better if there were ten people here' we find ourselves at the other end of the scale. It is quite feasible to contradict such a statement, but not on the strength of its untruth. Value judgments are appealing or unappealing: they may be *highly* objectionable, but they cannot be falsified. Everyone is his own authority if it is the custom to appeal to authorities where normative statements are concerned. Value judgments are subject to what a methodological anarchist (Paul Feyerabend) once wrongly said about the scientific method: 'anything goes'.

Most economists accept that normative statements cannot be falsified. Nevertheless, a problem remains here for the convinced ethician. For such a person can maintain that normative statements of a decidedly bad or criminal nature can most definitely be subjected to the above criterion of untruth: 'anybody who says that is not right in the head'. This verdict is applicable if certain limits are exceeded. Anyone who believes that two plus two is five is making a joke or is crazy; the same applies to anyone who advocates that one can beat one's neighbour to death for the fun of it. And yet it's a different kind of joke and a different kind of craziness. 'Untrue' is not the same as 'bad', though it isn't easy to explain this difference exactly. Fortunately, this is hardly a consideration for economists. The normative statements that economists tend to make can be contradicted by others, or conjure up a feeling of antipathy, or even the verdict: 'anyone who contends that is an immoral person' – but they are not so extreme that one charges one's opponent with having lost his reason. It is my personal opinion that callousness towards people with very low incomes points to a pretty unattractive character, but I shan't regard someone who evinces that callousness as insane. Anyone who insists that two plus two is five incurs that suspicion.

The basis of this essay is that in economics there is a scale of statements with falsifiability as the criterion. We may say of some statements: that is very probably true, that is definitely not true; but that is difficult with other ones, and is out of the question with other statements again. It is my contention that we can have a better understanding of this scale by dividing these statements into seven categories. It may well be feasible to make a similar classification with more than seven categories, but I maintain that a smaller number gives less insight. Seven is a commendable number – that is a piece of methodological advice belonging to category No. 7.

In the next chapter these seven categories are summarized. Then the empty boxes are filled to some extent in the sense that an impressionistic diagnosis is given of the degree of general agreement and disagreement within each category. The guiding thought is of course that uncertainty and unfalsifiability lead to divergent points of view. There is the uncomfortable feeling that if two are bickering at least one is wrong and probably both (Descartes). Indeed, some debates point to ignorance. The current difference of opinion about the question whether underspending prevails in a given country at a given moment points to a deficiency in our measurements. By improving the statistics we can make progress, and one of the two parties in the debate may perhaps become convinced of the plausibility of his opponent's viewpoint. But economics is characterized by quite different disagreements, of the kind that do not necessarily evaporate through better observation, better logic or better econometrics. The examples are to be found in the field of selective observation, Gestalt, colligation and storytelling. In that field two people stating the opposite can both be right. We find them not only among Great Thinkers; within the corporate culture too debates are going on that are based on different stories. Such a debate can last a long time. I do not say that there is no solution for this. But it will have to come from somewhere that has been inadequately mapped by our textbooks. Rhetoric is involved, and moral argumentation, and attempts to affect each other's subconscious.

It is above all the latter problems that have inspired this essay. I have an idea that economic science is trying to push these things outside its field proper, as being too journalistic, too soft, slightly suspect, full of value judgments, ideology and demagogy. I shall argue that this puristic point of view can very well be defended – economists can withdraw to areas where statements can be made with certainty and disagreements have finally to disappear. But my own choice is different. I am an advocate of a warm kind of economics (5).

(1)Whilst I am writing this the nearly 900-page *Economics* by Martin Bronfenbrenner, Werner Sichel and Wayland Gardner (Boston, 1984) is published. It closely resembles Samuelson, though all the same it is rather special. There are pictures in it of great economists, and of a soup kitchen in the Thirties, but no illustrations of the stock exchange, a well-known government building, a facsimile of the frontispiece of the *Wealth of Nations* or *The General Theory of Employment, Interest and Money,* which happens nowadays. Bronfenbrenner et al. write on p. vii: 'We believe that a beginning text should be (1) open-minded and searching for the best in all schools of thought where there is disagreement, (2) thorough and realistic in presenting material that is generally accepted, and (3) flexible and oriented to a broad view in matters like international trade, economic development, and comparative economic systems'. Nevertheless, it is not a book on pure economic logic; it contains a substantial number of references to reality, descriptions and stories. Policy recommendations are successfully avoided – although 'too much waste will be dumped in places where property rights are not established' .... 'so, to get the best balance among the different methods of waste disposal, governments must work with private companies' (p. 718).

I do in fact believe that almost everything in this fat book may be described as 'generally accepted'. That is quite a lot. And we can multiply the volume further by a factor $x$, where $x$ depends on the amount of formal logic that we want to have along. But there are also fields where dissension reigns; and these are not spotlighted by the usual textbook. Bronfenbrenner et al. are no exception to this rule.

(2)In particular: *Welvaartstheorie en economische politiek*, edited by J. van den Doel and A. Heertje, Alphen aan den Rijn, Brussels, 1977.
(3)G.J. Stigler, *The Economist as Preacher and other Essays*, Chicago, Oxford, 1982. The author proffers various explanations for the ineffectuality of economists; one reason is that a theory can usually support various policy prescriptions.
(4)The way in which political preferences penetrate economic theory has been described in pioneering fashion by Gunnar Myrdal, *Das Politische Element in der Nationaloekonomischen Doktrinbildung*, 1932. He pointed inter alia to the norm-laden character of the terminology. But he also wrote: 'The technology of economics .... can help to keep the political struggle more honest' (English edition, London, 1953, p. 206). In fact the latter sentence is the moral of my essay, be it that the stress is on can. If economists have an immoral view of their task, they make the political disputes greater. And vice versa.
(5)I therefore feel a certain fleeting sympathy for the set-up of that remarkable book by Ken Cole, John Cameron and Chris Edwards, *Why Economists Disagree, The Political Economy of Economics*, London and New York, 1983. They see three large schools: the conservatives, the social democrats and the 'socialists', which seems to me a fruitful starting point, and they seek the economic basis of these trends. The authors seek that basis in the theory of value. The conservatives embrace the subjective preference theory, the social democrats the cost of production theory and the socialists the abstract labour theory. This link between the theory of value and all other concepts is extremely weak – it makes the thought pattern of these authors a forced one. Much worse is that Cole, Cameron and Edwards have a bizarre view of what they call the social democratic school. They hate this school in a way that one would not think possible: 'a managerial ideology, capable of delivering to a deprived minority of us what a well-educated minority feels they need. At one extreme, it is muddled, benign and well-meaning if ineffective, at the other it is arrogant, manipulative, and authoritarian if, in some narrow sense, efficient' (p. 190). This then refers to the Keynesians, the Galbraithians, the whole political centre. It will not surprise the reader that my slight sympathy for the methodological point of departure turns into a certain disgust. Cole et al. try to break up the political spectrum with economic arguments, so that only the extremes – the conservatives and the Marxists – remain. This immoral nature of the book is also reflected in the view that 'all theories are correct in so far as they further sectional interests' (p. 15). This illustrates that the gentlemen are not interested in the truth. The book stinks.

Chapter II

## SEVEN TYPES OF STATEMENTS

The following classification, which is the backbone of this essay, summons up the usual problems: are the bulkheads between the compartments watertight? Do overlaps exist? Do the statements affect one another reciprocally, so that the whole taxonomic exercise is rather futile? I therefore hasten to say that the following is intended as a typology, rough at the edges, not without overlaps. In the case of some assertions it may be doubted in which box they belong. 'There was a fatal crisis in 1929'; is that an observation or a small story? But I believe that the categories are recognizable enough to encourage economists to ponder the question: what am I trying to say?

### 2.1. Statements on observables

Observing is something we do with our senses, of which we have five. Economics is mostly concerned with looking, although in some topical disagreements the sense of smell is involved: environmental problems are controversial. Many economic phenomena are directly observable: a car, the number of cars in a country, the number of persons in a country. But the number of persons owning a car cannot be ascertained by looking at them – the observer has to ask questions. The interest rate laid down in a given contract may seem a simple observable number, but it cannot be seen or felt or smelled. You can look at the contract, but then you see a piece of paper with letters and figures on it, and you have to perform a mental operation of no small complexity to answer the question: what is the interest rate? You can also look at the number of monetary units that passes from the borrower to the lender when the interest is due, but it is not always easy to interpret what you perceive. And this certainly applies to an 'observable' like somebody's income; it is the outcome of a bookkeeping operation. More generally speaking, observation is not just a matter of 'opening the doors of perception' – the observer is engaged in a highly complex mental activity. Moreover, observation is always subject to the condition that the observer is in a favourable position and is well equipped, if necessary with instruments (spectacles, measuring equipment). That condition is not always met. Non-repeatable facts from the past can no longer be observed, and the past is rather extensive. We rely on what others have observed and written down – that creates many potential complications, but it works out better than one might expect in economics. In the event of a difference of opinion renewed observation or renewed study of historical sources must establish who is right.

Economic observables can often be measured, and observing is then measuring. Statistics is the vast and rather solid ground on which the house of economics is built. Some confusion and conflict may occur in the calculation of averages: index numbers, ratios. This takes us still further away from direct observation. It is defensible to deal with these numbers, including even the GNP, under this category. But strictly speaking the GNP is a colligative concept: a fiction or even a story.

As regards the importance of measuring, a methodological disagreement is raging between the subcultures. Some economists are of the opinion that we cannot really understand a phenomenon unless we can quantify it. The view is ascribed to Lord Kelvin and is defended by Tinbergen and other econometricians. Other economists are more accommodating and believe that much of our knowledge is of a quantitative nature. A third tendency reverses Kelvin's opinion. Something that is valuable cannot be expressed in figures: Christmas, a love letter (1). I recommend the second school of thought, with the proviso that it seems to me desirable to move the dividing line between the qualitative and the quantitative upward as far as possible. The more numbers the better. They will improve the quality of the stories we tell and the judgments we make. Suppose that we could measure a love letter (in terms of input, output, effect on the recipient) – what a forward leap in our knowledge ...

It is tempting to label only observations as facts, and therefore to regard as a fact only that which in principle can be observed by the senses. However, that is at variance with common usage. Someone (for instance L. Robbins) says: 'it is a fact that subjects order their wants in accordance with their intensity'. However, that is not an observation but a fiction. Someone else says: 'it is a fact that

economists like to use metaphors'. That is not an observation either, unless one interprets the reading of the book in
which the metaphors occur as a sensory process – a somewhat forced opinion. Or someone says: 'it is a fact that economics is about people'. These three 'facts' are not observations. Confusion occurs when we precede statements on
unobservable facts by an appeal to sensory observations:
'Look, economics is about people' (2). The word 'look' is
a rhetorical artifice, for there is nothing to be seen. A similar trick consists in someone beginning a sentence with 'It
is a fact that ...', followed by something that is neither observable nor true. The four assertions cited (by Robbins,
Pen, and Pen) are at best half-truths. My terminological
conclusion is that there is no objection to our interpreting
the word 'observation' rather broadly, but that we must
watch out with the word 'fact'. Better avoid it (3).

In what follows the proposition will be defended that
economists have at their disposal a tremendous number of
observations, and that there is also a considerable consensus on them. There are exceptions to this rule – I shall list
five cases in which our observations are defective, so that
differences of opinion arise about our basic material. Those
differences of opinion have consequences; they may even
spread like wildfire if we proceed to tell stories – about the
depression, about the environment etc. – for a difference of
opinion never comes unaccompanied.

But then it will be argued that defective information is
one thing and selective observation something else. The latter creates debates at a low intellectual level. People talk at
cross-purposes, and it may be extremely difficult to estab-

lish who is right. While defective observation can in principle be improved by more information, and especially by more statistical work, selective observation tends to thrive if the basic material increases. There is then a greater freedom for the observer to select. The one set of data is considered relevant and the other not. What one chooses depends of course on the story that one wishes to tell – and that introduces a remarkable element into the debate. 'That isn't relevant', the debater cries, and who shall say him nay? An example will be given of this rhetorical practice too: income distribution, a source of heated debate.

## 2.2. Logical statements

They are arrived at by pure reasoning. That is something that people can do. They do it without ever being taught how to derive logical propositions. It is actually quite astonishing. One has never studied the rules of logic, never heard of truth functions, quantification theory and the theory of equality. One has never read W.V. Quine, *Methods of Logic* (London, 1952). The mysterious expression, $\forall x P(x) \vee \exists x \neg P(x)$, in which $\exists$ is an existential quantifier and $\forall$ is a universal quantifier, inspires a vague feeling of being cut off from some deeper insight, but certainly does not illuminate the workings of one's own mind. Still, one goes on reasoning just as one goes on breathing. Economists are like other people when it comes to logic – they practise it without theory. They're even very good at it. Perhaps not as good as mathematicians, but some economists come close to them. Much of the subject of economics – according to some, the whole subject ! – consists of cleverly derived propositions, which sometimes may be very surprising and exciting. Disagreements on logical propositions have a special property – the opposite party is put down as stupid. That is the result of the imperative nature of the logic. Someone constructs a line of reasoning, and anyone who thinks differently about it is guilty of false reasoning. False observation can be debated with a certain good temper, but anyone guilty of false reasoning must recognize that. If not, obstinacy is piled on stupidity.

It is in fact my opinion that disagreements on logical statements are usually short-lived. Economists have at their disposal a large arsenal of logic, and compared to that the unsettled logical disputes are few in number. I shall list below a handful of propositions on which there is a consensus, but solely as an example – a full list requires a very fat book. Samuelson's *Foundations* contains a number of such propositions, but only some of them. Anyone who likes to think that economists agree on many matters must withdraw into this castle. It's a pretty secure place, though not quite as secure as it used to be.

That is then typically the world of the textbooks. A 'dry' economics textbook is confined to logical propositions, their derivations and their graphical illustrations. Especially since model-building became fashionable, the subject-matter has been abundantly available. Walrasian equilibrium, Keynesian underspending, consumer's choice, the golden rule of growth, the optimum under linear constraints – it can all be described exactly and elegantly. This is necessary in order to understand the world, but of course it is not a sufficient condition. More knowledge has to be presented, otherwise we remain caught in the self-sufficiency of logic.

For that's the danger of pure logic; it creates a certain euphoria. We've grasped it. We draw three straight lines and we know national income at given capital investment and a given consumption function. We draw two curves and we have the IS-LM model. We write down a production function and we know what the distribution of income between labour and capital looks like.

The misunderstanding that logic provides us with genuine knowledge of reality is strengthened by the misuse of the word 'theory'. We write down the neo-classical rules of growth, in which the strategic coefficients are represented by Greek letters, and say that we have a theory of growth. That is not so. We do not have a theory until we have produced a set of falsifiable hypotheses, and logic may certainly help us in that direction, but the final decisive steps are taken by empirical research. The Greek letters must refer at least to constant quantities, and these must preferably be determined numerically. If they remain variable we do not have a theory. This may sound trivial, but every day economists speak of theories that are not theories but sets of logical propositions – just as they speak of facts that are not facts but rhetorical exclamations.

However, there are worse things than the euphoria of logic. More confusing is the fact that logic can conjure up very different worlds for us. While there is considerable consensus about that logic itself, there is anything but consensus about the reality of these worlds. Logic is like the railways: trains are heading in every direction. There is a chance that someone knows only one line and regards the rest of the timetable as unimportant. Others take another line and arrive at quite a different destination. They lose sight of each other. That happens to economists.

Another consequence is that logic plays a great part in colligation: creating images and telling stories. It would be a misunderstanding to think that colligation is based solely on bold exclamations, metaphors, well-chosen instances; it usually contains a load of logic. Whether this leads to the truth is a question for empirical research.

### 2.3. Empirical statements

These are the genuine theories: explanations of reality. They form the heart of science. They are based on a peculiar combination of logic and observation backing one another. The statements concern relations between observable events.

The empirical statements of economists are, unfortunately, rather controversial. Formerly one tried to prove one's point by referring to facts that seemed to confirm one's favourite views. This practice has fallen into dispute since Popper, but is still frequently applied in popular discussions. The Popperian method, which regards theories as hypotheses that can be falsified, leaves a special mark on science. The latter advances through a process of conjectures and refutations. The discussion then assumes the form that rival hypotheses are rejected. This is something that the supporters of those hypotheses rarely accept. The true scientist is even supposed to challenge his own favourite theory. The Popperian method breathes scepticism and leads inevitably to dispute. Empirical economics, or econometrics, is full of uncertainties, hesitations. In this sense it is the exact opposite of the world of logic, where self-assurance reigns. And it cannot be denied: a fairly considerable measure of disagreement occurs among economic empiricists.

For the connections between the variables must be established not only in terms of sign – that is usually feasible – but also numerically. Preferably in the form of parameters, i.e. constant regression coefficients. When economists quarrel, econometrics acts as referee. This cannot be reiterated enough: a genuine theory is not born until the econometricians have had a helping hand in the delivery. The numerical value of the parameters is an essential form of knowledge. These values determine what is *important* in our world and what is not. They determine the *structure* of reality, an essential concept in every form of scientific practice (4). Quantitative insight is also required if we tell a story. Accurate colligation requires reliable estimates of the parameters, and if econometrics is deficient colligation becomes a wild, controversial game.

Empirical statements are in essence predictions of what will happen under certain conditions. We do not have a genuine theory until we can predict. We do not understand the present unless we have at our disposal an ex post prediction that explains the available data from the past and extends the explanation to the future. 'Unpredicted is unexplained.' This methodological position is defended by strict methodologists, and we must sympathize with it (5).

This methodological requirement is often considered unbearably heavy – in that case there is no social science at all, I hear it said. After all, social and economic life is not predictable. I believe this to be a highly exaggerated view. Daily life is full of predictions, economic practice is full of predictions, and the strange thing is that they are often fulfilled. If we open the bathroom door, we expect to find something behind it that's there too – if we encounter a yawning abyss or a royal tiger the prediction is wrong, but that's a rare occurrence. The businessman who borrows from a bank knows that he has to pay interest, and he can more or less predict what will happen if he fails to meet his payments. A government that reduces taxes on income can expect that more is consumed. All these predictions are based on a complicated mental process, in which logic and observation are intertwined. It is never so that repeated observation leads to certainty – anyone who sees an old man pass by daily knows on the contrary for sure that the day will come when this will no longer happen. Every prediction is made by virtue of a theory; that is so in daily life, and in physics, and in economics. The theories that we use in daily life are no simpler than the economists' theories – on the contrary. The fact that nevertheless the economists' predictions work out so much more insecurely is a part of the weakness of economic structures. This is the central problem of economic science which, however, may never

lead to defeatism. (The latter is a value judgment, but then of a methodological nature – it belongs in category 2.7.)

## 2.4. Value judgments

These can be the subject of vigorous debate – *de gustibus est disputandum* – but there are no scientific methods for deciding who is right. We can, however, try to *convince* one another. But nobody need accept the referee's arguments (off the football field). 'I'm always right' is a tenable argument in this category. Which is a pity, because the value judgments affect the *image* that we form of ourselves and of the world we live in. Added to that, the question is what *convince* precisely means in ethics: appealing to an authority? To a book? Does it include brain-washing? Or the kind of rhetoric recommended at the end of this essay?

The popular discussion on economic subjects is principally a clash of value judgments, and little more. Low incomes have to be spared, taxes are too high, the budgetary deficit has to be reduced. A debate of this kind is often regarded as a debate among economists. Perhaps that is the Great Popular Misunderstanding. It is a debate among human beings. But, because economists are human beings, they adhere to value judgments. The latter penetrate their scientific activities, a trivial proposition that some scientists refuse to accept. Economists should be aware of the ethical and moral implications of their views. A disquieting idea for the positivists, but still worth considering.

## 2.5. Colligation

This is the interweaving of selective observation, well-aimed logic, empirical statements and value judgments into an image, a view or a story. Everyone – historian, sociologist, economist, psychologist, politician, citizen – is involved in colligation, but the stories differ. The one is more credible than the other, but how do we determine that? We can try again to convince one another, and science certainly has a task, but what exactly? (6)

It looks as if this arbitral role is the same as that under 2.1, 2.2 and 2.3: once again establishing what the observable facts are, reasoning as well as possible, approaching the empirical relations as honestly as possible. The latter task falls to econometrics, and it has already been remarked above that uncertainty regarding the numerical values of the parameters is an excuse for unhindered colligation. What then happens is that the speaker implies parameters that give a decisive turn to his tale. Science can signal this but cannot give a proper verdict on the reliability of the reasoning.

However, something else happens in colligation than the interweaving of facts and logic and the implicit estimating of parameters. Images are conjured up, metaphors used; poetry is perpetrated. These rhetorical artifices have a considerable effect on the credibility of the story. However, it is difficult for economics as a science to verify their correctness. That is particularly the case with the metaphor, i.e. the use of a word or expression for something else than what it usually means. Perhaps that is not permitted in science – opinions differ on this issue, see below – but economists do it daily. The metaphor can have tremendous power of conviction, especially if we do not notice what is happening to us: that is to say, if the subconscious is affected. Then the world changes.

The rhetorical nature of economics is rarely brought up for discussion (an exception: Donald N. McCloskey, The Rhetoric of Economics, *Journal of Economic Literature*, June 1983, Vol. XXI, No. 2, p. 481), and if it does happen it arouses opposition. Understandable opposition, for rhetoric is usually regarded as something most unscientific. We have here a methodological controversy, which rarely finds proper expression: what are the advantages and disadvantages of colligation? We shall come back to this. However, one thing that is certain is that the use of imagery, metaphors and rhetorical artifices tends rather to hamper unequivocal arbitral statements on the question: who's right? What is truth?

## 2.6. Policy recommendations

These form a special case of the value judgments, namely measure *A* is better than measure *B*. This is the subject of violent dispute, which attracts attention; outsiders believe that it is a scientific contest. On further consideration citizens are debating with one another, and the squabble may well be the result of differences in objectives. These objectives are based on value judgments. But at the same time there are scientific elements in the policy discussion, namely the diagnosis of the actual situation and the prediction of the effect of measures. It has been endeavoured (by Tinbergen and others) to treat policy advice analytically as a combination of (a) choice of the objectives, which is the citizen's responsibility, and (b) choice of instruments, a task for science. This bipartition is fruitful as long as we bear in mind firstly that neutral instruments hardly exist, secondly that the decision model is constantly the subject of controversy and thirdly that policy recommendations are always made in a context of colligation. We shall come back to this matter.

All citizens, including economists, have a tendency to harmonize their view of society and the policy recommendations that they favour. This is done by implicitly adapting the parameters of the model to what one wants to get out of it. All this makes policy advice a form of normative supercolligation, in which everyone tends to remain convinced that he is right.

## 2.7. *Methodological statements*

This is – I hate to say it – a field in which confusion is rife. I myself for a long time mixed up three questions (until J.J. Klant corrected me), namely: How do economists set about understanding the world? How do economists think that they set about understanding the world? How must economists set about understanding the world?

The answer to that first question calls for serious study of the literature (in this essay it is assumed that the reader has already performed that study, so that incidental references will suffice). But the books and the articles are only an output, and do not always betray the secrets of the production process. The way of thinking remains concealed, for instance when positivists keep the creative and poetic elements in their work in the background and describe only the formal procedures that they followed in their research. Come to that, it is not so very easy to find out how people think – the more you ponder it, the less possible it becomes. The thought process is one of nature's most closely guarded secrets.

The second question, i.e. how economists think that they think, summons up all the questions of the self-image. The cool expert, feeding his data into the computer, will look up in wonder when somebody turns up with a tale about storytelling – perhaps he'll accept it as a mild joke, but if he's in a bad mood he'll prefer not to listen to it. Selective observation, one of the vulnerable spots in an economist's intellectual life, is rarely recognized as a correct description of one's own thought process: it's usually the others who do that. And the fact that someone, in the construction of his model, reasons in the direction of a political conclusion is a sharp reproach, but that doesn't make it any the less true. Some economists are paid to think something up that fits in with the interests of whoever is paying. There's nothing criminal about that, but all the same it doesn't fit into the self-image.

That is because the third question is always involved: how should economists think? What rules should they follow? This normative question is always in the foreground

if we ask someone about his thought processes, or if he
makes spontaneous statements. Usually the normative
question displaces the first two factual questions; methodological dissertations on economics describe the rules of the
game and the way in which others break those rules. Unfortunately, differing answers are given to the normative
question about the best method. The opponent is accused
not only of wrong conclusions but also of wrong methods.
All this together makes a minefield of methodological discussion. Most economists prefer to detour round it.

Now I say that we can't do that. We are walking in that
minefield, and we can do it with open or closed eyes. That
is not to say that I recommend the extensive reading of
methodological works (7). But I feel that economists must
be aware of at least one methodological problem, and that
is their attitude to colligation and political engagement.
Everyone has to make a choice between the cool and the
warm approach, and the chapter 'Methodological statements' is concerned with that choice. The moral question
is an old chestnut, which we simply can't get rid of. My assertion is that we are confronted there with a pretty free
choice, something that economists should find agreeable.
My own preference is for the warm approach, as will be argued in Chapter XII. But it is a good thing that others will
choose differently. In this case, pluriformity is to be recommended, and so is tolerance.

The above survey of seven types of statements has served
its purpose if the reader has become convinced that the
search for truth takes place in seven different ways. Disputes about observables are different in nature from logical

disputes – the latter are fiercer, because the opposite party is suspected of false reasoning. The procedure for admitting that someone is right is also different; the technique for ascertaining old and current observables is quite different from the strict application of logic. In the verification of empirical statements yet other techniques are involved: econometrics, and the disagreements have a different atmosphere, more difficult, less certain, more of a discourse between specialists. With value judgments anyone can join in, and science is not a referee. Colligation is perhaps the most interesting and the most slippery category; the temperature is higher and the results more uncertain. The same applies to the supercolligation of policy advice: very hot, and the question is how we can lower the temperature there. The discussion on the method will certainly go on indefinitely, and in that discussion different approaches can exist side by side without biting each other.

What has to be done next is to give an impression within each of the seven categories of the current mix of consensus and dissension.

(1) W. Roepke, The Place of Economics among the Sciences in: *On Freedom and Free Enterprise, Essays in Honor of L. von Mises*, 1956, p. 122–123.

(2) The first sentence of a picture book. J. Pen, *Kijk, Economie*. Utrecht, Antwerp, 1979.

(3) The word 'fact' is used differently by philosophers. Some claim that it should be reserved for something that is *certain* and is therefore not subject to any controversy. In this spirit C. Perelman and L. Olbrechts-Tyteca, *The New Rhetoric*, London 1969. 'Fact' and 'truth' are close approximations of each other, and this essay could be called: 'How many facts have economists at their disposal, and what are their non-facts?' Perhaps we may then say that facts are: two times two is four; real incomes in

Western Europe were higher in 1984 than in 1950; an elasticity is the ratio
between the marginal and average quantity; most British adults occasionally drink tea; mass unemployment is a bad thing. Personally I consider
this usage rather strange, because these 'facts' are of an extremely heterogeneous nature. They include value judgments, statements of pure logic,
statements on numbers based on observation. Incidentally, it is then not
a fact that unemployment is a bad thing, for a growing number of contemporaries are of the opinion that paid work is bad for a human being. In
the case of other philosophers the fact precedes knowledge: the pure truths
of mathematics. This is in conflict with usage. Still other philosophers
(Husserl) make it even more difficult and regard the *Tatsache* as something accidental, to be distinguished from the *Wesen*. The disagreement
among philosophers on this point surpasses that among economists.
(4)Structure is an essential concept in the social sciences, but unfortunately the word is used in a variety of meanings. That becomes evident when
we ask what the opposite is. Some sociological authors set structure
against function, others against process, others again against the things
that vary. I should like to associate myself with the latter. In anthropology
structure is regarded as something deeper and invisible, opposed to the
manifest. Structure always points to order, but sometimes this order is
pure regularity, a pattern, without permanence. In that case one speaks
of changing structures, which I find confusing. Some authors regard the
structure as a beautiful thing, associated with harmony and consensus,
but others see a threat in it: man is dehumanized by the structures. For
political observers of the far left a structure is something that has to be
blown up, preferably by dynamite. Biologists will remark that no life is
possible without structure. To a structuralist like Lévi-Strauss the structure is something lying deeply below the surface, but it is difficult to determine what exactly he means by that. To Foucault human beings are nodal
points in the structures, and therefore he is of the opinion that people do
not in fact exist. Thought is therefore an anonymous process.

It is the habit of economists to contrast the structure with the 'conjunc-
ture', but the distinction is not always clear. They also use structure for
the quantitative relationship between agriculture, industry and service sector. This usage seems too narrow to me.

In my view the structure is the constant element in a changing world.
We observe many variables, and those variables do what variables always
do, namely vary, but among them there exist – let us hope – constant relations. These can be described by a model, and therefore the structure can
be defined as the *form of the model and the numerical value of the parame-*

*ters.* This concept of structure stems from econometrics. It is the task of econometrics to track down the structures. But every structure is provisional: it is a set of Popperian hypotheses, always awaiting refutation. Anyone who believes that economic structures do not exist sees nothing in econometrics. Someone like that falls back on economic logic and then lapses into unconfined colligation. Or into silence. I consider this a saddening solution.

(5)This strict rule is defended by C.G. Hempel and P. Oppenheim (Studies in the Logic of Explanation, in C.G. Hempel, ed., *Aspects of Scientific Explanation,* New York, 1948, p. 245). The predictability of economic events is challenged by many scholars, including G.L.S. Shackle, *Epistemics and Economics, A Critique of Economic Doctrines,* Cambridge, 1973. Shackle is of the opinion that economic science can merely enumerate possible results, but cannot pronounce on the probability with which they will occur, as a result of given causes. The uncertainty is too great. It is my opinion that this scepticism goes much too far. Not only is economic science dropped overboard – that is not the worst of it – but every form of practical action becomes a leap in the dark. Whatever happens, nothing need surprise us. The concept 'potential surprise', introduced into economics by Shackle himself, becomes meaningless. If I come across a full-grown tiger sitting in my bathroom playing a Bach cello suite, I may classify the situation, but surprise is not permitted. Life isn't like that, nor is economic policy. There a large degree of predictability fortunately prevails.

(6)Colligation is a term from the debate between historians. It can be taken to mean a thought process – what goes on in the historian's brain – or the statements that result from of the process. That result is also called *narrative.* This essay is concerned with colligatory statements, and how we can establish whether they are correct. The concept 'colligation' has been brought to the fore above all by W.H. Walsh, for instance in his article *Colligatory Concepts in History* in P. Gardiner, ed.: *The Philosophy of History,* Oxford, 1974. A stimulating book is F.R. Ankersmit, *Narrative Logic, A Semantic Analysis of the Historian's Language,* The Hague, Boston, London, 1983. If economists talk about these things they often do so by means of Benjamin Ward: *What is Wrong with Economics* (London, 1972) who introduced the concept of colligation into economics and is in favour of it.

(7)It is for instance highly discouraging to take cognizance of the debate set going by Milton Friedman on the question of the extent to which the realism of assumptions is relevant. Friedman has defended the mysterious proposition that this is not the case – assumptions are irrelevant, as long as the result of the reasoning is capable of explaining reality. Occasionally Friedman has even hinted that it would be a virtue if assumptions were to be of a highly unrealistic nature. This appears in the *Essay on the Methodology of Positive Economics* (Chicago, 1953). This kind of attitude makes methodology a discouraging business. Fortunately, the idea has disappeared in the interim.

Chapter III

# DEFECTIVE OBSERVATION

Economists have formidable amounts of observations at their disposal. The statistical offices of every country work hard. They publish the material in great flows. In addition, there are massive data banks in the corporate subculture. In part these are micro-data, which may be regarded as near observations: figures on individual prices, incomes, physical yields per hectare, production volumes. In part the data are summarized in generally accepted averages: the wages of British miners. In part they are macro-figures, such as national income, total proceeds of taxation. In this list we are drawing further and further away from direct observation. The raw material is being increasingly cooked. An element of colligation is creeping in, and with it a possible disagreement.

There may be doubt about the exact meaning of aggregates and macro-figures. For instance, a sceptic may maintain that the National Product is a fiction, representing not a single observable reality; since in the course of time the composition of the product changes, there is no possible deflator that justifies the step from nominal national income to real income. (This was in fact Keynes' own point of view; real output cannot be measured.) Despite all this potential scepticism, the argument that the major disagree-

ments are not to be found here seems justified. Most observations are accepted as facts, and the operations that the
statisticians perform are welcomed with a certain confidence. Thanks to Simon Kuznets and many others. The
view that there are lies, damned lies and statistics is not endorsed by the profession.

The rule that figures are uncontroversial is subject to exceptions, which in part are trivial, and in part not. A trivial
exception concerns data from old times. National income
can be estimated only for recent periods, and calculating
back requires a certain heroism. Angus Maddison (1) is
good at that: real per capita income has risen in the United
States since 1820 by a factor of 16, and in the United
Kingdom by a factor of 9. These are rather strong pronouncements, all methodological scepticism notwithstand-
ing. Historians naturally debate among themselves, and
this leads to a constant improvement of our knowledge, but
this is not a cause for deep concern among economists.

Another trivial aspect is that various subdivisions of the
contemporary material are inadequate. Exports of some
goods are unknown, above all where military production
is concerned. This can hardly be called an essential gap in
our general knowledge, although it will distress those who
are interested in peace, security and the role of the industrial military complex. The data on income distribution
also leave something to be desired – for instance, we cannot
sufficiently perfect Paul Taubman's attempts to measure
the effect of personal factors on income. Longitudinal series for the income of individuals are in short supply. The
constant call for better statistics is therefore self-evident,

but these holes in our knowledge do not lead to serious controversies.

However, there are at least five exceptions to this rule. Important inadequacies in our statistical information, which lead to unresolved controversies.

Firstly, little is known about the environment and environmental pollution. We are concerned here with an observable variable, and in themselves the observations are not scarce. Throughout the world environmental statistics are being built up. In the Netherlands this work is being done at the Central Bureau of Statistics under the direction of Roefie Hueting. But the data are of a physical nature and thus are fragmentary. They cannot be placed under a common denominator because the shadow prices are unknown and controversial. We know something about the salt content of the ground water, about sulphur dioxide in the atmosphere, about heavy metals in the ground and about chlorinated hydrocarbons. The areas where poisonous chemicals were dumped have been provisionally mapped. But a summarizing verdict on the situation is impossible, as a result of which differing opinions exist on the seriousness of the situation. Some observers report reassuringly on salmon that have returned to the Thames and on the disappearance of London's smog. Others point to acid rain and the disappearance of the forests. Hope and fear determine the picture. Opinions are formed against the background of nuclear energy and nuclear weapons – this stirs up emotions. Moreover, the problem is a worldwide one – pessimists think of Harrisburg or the deforestation in Latin America. The logic of the doom scenarios is a ready vehicle for translating these emotions into computer output. We encounter here one of the latest sources of controversy, and one of the most fundamental. I do not say that uniformity of the predictions would be obtainable if we had better environmental data – the world is too large for that and the possibilities of cognitive dissonance are too generously present – but it is clear that a lack of statistics forms a serious handicap for our insight.Unfortunately no immediate improvement is in sight, because the data are not commensurable.

A second gap in our knowledge. The size of the 'black' sector is not properly known, for obvious reasons. There are estimates ranging for the various countries from five to perhaps twenty-five percent of national income. That would not be so bad – except perhaps that we lack one more moral criterion for measuring general degeneration – but it obscures diagnosis of the recession. According to some observers the recession of the Eighties is less than it seems. Ed Feige in particular has posited that the depression is a false observation: according as official production stagnated, people sought refuge in the unobserved sector, which is flourishing. We are quite a bit better off than the statistical offices and the politicians say (2). This argument can form a springboard for a whole tale about people's inventivity, the resilience of the market sector and the needless pessimism of the Keynesian view – in brief, colligation on the basis of uncertainty about the facts observed. Personally, I don't believe Feige's story because I have more confidence than he in the unemployment statistics; figures of about ten percent most certainly point to unutilized capacity. The production estimates of the Central Bureau of Statistics are also better than Feige suggests, because a part of the black circuit is definitely taken into account in them. But what matters is that here we encounter a gap in our knowledge of the observable facts, as a result of which rather different opinions come about.

Thirdly. Profits are a strategic form of income, because they act as the incentive and the principal source of financing for investment in capital goods. In principle this quantity is measurable, but we encounter many problems. At the level of the individual firm the question already arises which figure must be entered for depreciation – in times of technological turbulence and shifting sales patterns traditional methods of writing-off are inadequate, and the management must ask what the real decline in capital value has been. Next, it makes a difference whether the interest on one's capital resources has to be counted as a cost factor. In the case of small businesses the question arises how the entrepreneur's labour should be valued. In the macro-economic profit figures all this can lead to different results. These are consequently uncertain – as regards both their absolute value and their share in national income. For instance, I have made calculations for Dutch profits in the late Seventies that justify both an after-tax share of 8% in national income and a negative figure (3). Thereafter the figures have become even more unfavourable.

This statistical uncertainty means that essential building blocks in our picture of the world remain insecure. A view exists that since the beginning of the Seventies, or even earlier, a profit squeeze has been going on. This is then claimed to be responsible in turn for the declining solvency of the enterprises, for the stagnating investments and for the recession which ultimately resulted in the depression of the Eighties. But others ascribe the recession and the depression to other factors in which profits play a less crucial role; more effect, less cause.

Quite apart from this topical question, profits are of great importance to our view of society. Frank Knight long ago pointed out that the level of profits is overestimated by everyone – *business as a whole suffers a loss,* was his opinion in 1921. And a recent researcher, William Nordhaus, noted that 'the corporate sector experienced essentially no net profitability', and that during a period, from 1948 to 1968, in which the American economy was nevertheless flourishing quite well. Nordhaus describes this result as 'most surprising' (4). And indeed this picture is in sharp contrast to the popular idea that profits form a considerable part of national income – twenty percent? Fifty percent?

That popular idea is nurtured by direct observations – in the field of conspicuous consumption and above all conspicuous architecture. The modern metropolis is dominated by the imposing buildings of big business, and that sight automatically leads thoughts to the profits from which all that has been paid. Come to that, the old commercial cities – Amsterdam, Venice, London – were built on profits. Many a tall story about capitalism is based on an implicit estimate of this special income category – and if that estimate is wrong, the story is no good. An unsolved puzzle?

Fourthly. The productive capacity of a country is not exactly known. This lack of knowledge does not particularly matter for some problems: anyone desirous of explaining international differences in real income may confine himself to the volume of production and need not worry about the potential output possible at a given moment. But the question of overcapacity rears its head as soon as we wish to diagnose the expenditure situation in a country, i.e. as soon as we raise the question whether more could not be produced if total demand were higher. Now this overcapacity is an important number in disputes about the policy to be followed. It proves to be a controversial quantity. It is defined as the capacity that could be profitably used at the given prices of inputs and outputs if there were more demand. It is already evident from this definition that perhaps we are hardly concerned with a directly observable quantity – there is a fictional element in it, something from the realm of Vaihinger's *Als-ob*. And yet someone who knows a business well can estimate the additional production that could be made in that business without a real expansion of capacity, and only by utilizing additional labour and additional raw materials. The official statistics on overcapacity are therefore based on surveys among the enterprises themselves. But they are of dubious significance, because it can always be maintained that the managers directly involved overestimate their possibilities – the machines are in reality outmoded, the workers have lost their skills, and moreover the prices are in fact too low to render profitable sales possible.

The result of this uncertainty about a quantity that is more or less observable is that the dispute continues to rage between the Keynesians, who say that there was a defi-

ciency of demand in the Seventies and Eighties, and the
supply-siders, who refuse to accept that. The diagnosis of
the recession and the depression depends on this question.
And connected with this are issues concerning the policy to
be followed – Keynesian or not. Here too it is true that
more factual information would hardly cause the controversy to vanish into thin air, but it would nevertheless be
welcome.

Fifthly. One of the central variables in economic thought
is the satisfaction of wants, summoned up by scarce resources. Or its complement: the difference between a person's wants and the satisfaction of those wants. This is a
highly individual, subjective phenomenon. It is not observable from outside. What we are in fact observing is whether
someone looks cheerful, or content, but there may be all
kinds of reasons for that which are detached from the avail-
ability of scarce resources. The utility gauge that some are
yearning for (others consider it a dreadful idea) has not yet
been invented. The data that we have – and they have recently become abundantly available, above all thanks to
the efforts of B.M.S. van Praag, A. Kapteyn et al. – are
based on opinion polls, that is to say on introspection (5).
Someone gives an account of his internal state of affairs,
but others cannot check that observation. This introduces
a controversial element into the discussion. People are asked what they think about their income, and what they think
about higher and lower incomes. From the answers welfare
functions are derived. One can be mindful of the great vir-
tues of this research work and still have some doubts about
its significance. The introspection that is translated into fig-

ures is nevertheless essentially different from 'real' measurement. Consequently Van Praag's conclusion that the greater part of the satisfaction of a growing real income is lost by the preference drift does not convince everyone. The idea elaborated by Kapteyn that a large portion of psychical income disappears because the next-door neighbour's income also rises will not convince everyone either. An increase in real income over long periods has immeasurable effects. Especially if we bear in mind that in the course of (recent!) history serious bottlenecks in the satisfaction of wants have been eliminated – i.e. overcoming poverty – a feeling of uncertainty creeps in. That is to say that some fundamental questions – is production growth good for the human race? – are left in the air. And those are precisely the questions that determine a person's view of the world.

These five examples – concerning the environment, the black sector, profits, underspending and people's welfare – show that something is lacking in our knowledge of observable or almost-observable quantities. Economists have an enormous amount of data at their disposal, and ignorance is more the exception that the rule. We should be impressed by the fact that statistical information on economic life is available en masse, and is steadily growing. Information technology is rushing ahead. The growth rate of the data banks is tremendous. The gaps in our knowledge are shrinking. However, some strategic forms of ignorance are still with us, and they are a source of disagreement. Moreover, all our statistical progress leaves another source of controversy intact, viz selective observation – our next topic.

(1)A. Maddison, *The Stages of Capitalist Development,* Oxford, 1982.

(2)E. Feige, Onzichtbare sector en markteconomie, *Economisch-Statistische Berichten,* 7 October, 1981. He speaks of the 'official muttering of the statistical offices'. A 'horde of economists' is sitting on the 'edge of the sick-bed' discussing the 'patient's crisis', but the patient is in better shape than the doctors believe.

(3)J. Pen, Profits as Rich Source of Puzzlement, *De Economist,* 128, No. 3, 1980.

(4)W. Nordhaus, The Falling Share of Profits, *Brooking Papers on Economic Activity,* 1974.

(5)B.M.S. van Praag, A. Kapteyn and F.G. van Herwaarden, The Individual Welfare Function of Income: a Lognormal Distribution Function, *European Economic Review,* Vol. 10, 1978, p. 395.

Chapter IV

## SELECTIVE OBSERVATION

Many debates between human beings are at a low level, even if they are concerned with observable things. Tom looks out of the window and says: 'I see a beautiful villa'. Dick testily remarks that Tom has got it all wrong – 'I see a slum'. Harry, who wants to reconcile the two parties, points to the presence of many, many council houses, and then gets into a row with Tom and Dick. They reproach each other with not seeing what is relevant. We could perhaps expect that economic science would manage to avoid such misunderstandings, but that is not so. Perhaps there are fewer anomalies inside economics than outside it, to the extent that economists possess a cool mentality, but scope remains for selective observation. There is no such thing as 'objectivity'. The debate on relevance is far from over. We have to bear in mind that this debate is essentially a moral debate. Let me mention as one of many examples personal income distribution.

Suppose that we know the incomes of everyone in a country. We have agreed who an income recipient is, for instance an individual and not a family (or vice versa); we include capital profits (or we don't). We know company profits; we assign them to individuals. Everything is crystal clear and our computer contains millions of data. More-

over, we have a complete time series: incomes are known
over a long series of years. Question: what about inequality
and how has it developed in time? Has it increased or de-
creased? There is no guarantee of a consensus on the answers. The one can claim that inequality is growing, the
other that there has been equalization. That depends on the
image that one has in mind.

One way of depicting the distribution is the graph, and
at least three graphs are possible. These are the frequency
distribution, the Lorenz concentration curve and the 'parade' of income recipients. They direct our attention towards various aspects of reality. They suggest different theoretical approaches. Even if people have never seen a
frequency distribution, a Lorenz curve or a fictitious parade, these concepts can still play a part in the stories that
are told – and, depend upon it, different stories are told
about the development of income distribution.

The frequency distribution clearly illustrates the inequality, but directs the observer's attention towards the mode.
The mode is closer to the low incomes than the high ones
– that is immediately evident. The arithmetic mean, and the
median, are to the right of the mode. The distribution is
evidently skew, other than the distribution of other human
properties, such as height. A criterion of skewness is the relative difference between mean and mode, and if this coefficient falls it will soon be concluded that equalization is occurring. The anomalies to the right – i.e. the rich – are there
in the picture, but faintly. There are so few really wealthy
people that they barely carry weight. Anyone who is used
to working with frequency distributions, and is then con-

fronted with an observer who claims that the absolute difference between the highest and the lowest (negative !) income presents an excellent picture of reality, will burst into
surprised laughter. (I have seen H. Theil do this – 'What?
The range?' he said.)

If in the course of time the mode becomes more densely
populated, the skewness lessens and the number of low incomes declines relatively, most economists will conclude
that a declining inequality is occurring, even if new anomalies should occur among the extremely high incomes.

The Lorenz curve diverts our view from the middle and
concentrates our attention on the extreme deciles. The top
ten percent get a given share, and that is on the decline. But
the bottom deciles do not see their share increase. On the
contrary, the extension of the welfare state can easily lead
to a decline. According as more citizens become entitled to
an income from social security or public assistance, while
those guaranteed incomes remain low, a drop in the lowest
shares of income may be expected. That is because the welfare state introduces into the data bank new income recipients who were not in it at first: jobless, old people, housewives, children. The welfare state leads to an optical en-
largement of inequality, which can be avoided by including
the new qualifiers for income in the old distribution with
a zero income, but this correction is hardly ever applied
and is regarded by some as irrelevant. Other times, other
manners, other rights, with the result that the share of the
bottom deciles is falling. The Lorenz curve therefore gives
some observers the idea that inequality is barely decreas-
ing, and they can be strengthened in this opinion if they

*Jan Pen*

consider the share of the top one percent, preferably before tax, in a country that is going through a boom with high profits. The observation must be carefully selected, and not too much attention must be paid to the Gini concentration index, which after all declines with the years, but such a selection is not forbidden.

Selective observation is definitely encouraged by the parade, whereby the height of the participants corresponds to their income. The observer, who is of average height, is struck by the large number of dwarfs, especially if the parade is being held in the welfare state (1). But at the same time the impression that the giants make on the observer is shattering. Preoccupation with these kilometre-tall persons may lead to the view that in the course of time no equalization in fact occurs. This view is at variance with what most economists think, but it does occur. The idea can be supported by considering the range of variation, and then preferably in absolute terms. That is to say that the simultaneous growth of all incomes, and even the purely nominal growth, leads by definition to an increase in inequality. These views occur in popular discussion, and often with a certain loudness. They appear to me to be not illogical, but 'unreasonable'. However, that is a value judgment, and the appeal to reason is in fact rhetorical. 'Improper' might be a better word – it stresses the moral character of the issue.

It is true that economists in general are more reasonable than the extreme commentators. They have devised criteria that try to present a summarizing overview of inequality. As the reader may know, the Theil coefficient is one of the best. It points to a stubborn continuation of equalization over the years, at least in the Western world. For the Netherlands a halving of the inequality may be noted between 1938 and the mid Seventies. There is a fairly considerable consensus on this view. Since then the process has continued, but in the Eighties a certain increase in income differentials has simultaneously occurred at the base between active and inactive members of the population.

The latter phenomenon – the recent cutbacks in social benefit – attracts the attention of those who disapprove of it (I am included among their number). The reduction in income transfers affects many old people, jobless and recipients of public assistance. Their real income is falling more strongly than that of the modal worker. The sad fact of the crumbling of the welfare state at the base is beginning to dominate the scene. For equalitarian commentators the Theil coefficient (which still points to equalization) is paling in the light of what is happening among the lowest incomes. That is selective observation. But is that forbidden? Is it forbidden to say that the cuts seem to me more relevant than the reduction in the income differential between three times modal income and typical income?

However, we can take a step further and maintain that the whole of income distribution is hardly relevant. Nobody can be forced on logical grounds to get worked up about this. It has sometimes been asserted, for instance by J.K. Galbraith in *The Affluent Society,* that preoccupation with these things is rather old-fashioned (but he wrote that in 1958: 'while it continues to have a large ritualistic role in the conventional wisdom of conservatives and liberals,

inequality has ceased to preoccupy men's minds'. It is not
entirely clear on what empirical research this conclusion
was based, nor whether Galbraith believed that this state
of mind would continue for a long time – it is a quotation
which he would probably prefer not to be reminded of).
Few will explicitly admit that they consider the distribution
irrelevant, but implicitly they act on this. Thus the OECD
utilizes a criterion for the economic performance of a
country in which four variables have been included: the
growth of GNP, the growth of productivity, the unemployment rate and the inflation rate. These four criteria are de-
picted in an extremely evocative image, in the shape of a
diamond. The size of this area can be well compared in respect of time, and so we see for instance a contraction of
the area over the period 1975–1983. The contraction would
have been greater, and the performance would have declin-
ed to a greater extent, if the distribution criterion had been
taken into account, with special regard to the low incomes;
certainly for the U.K. Here too we have an example of
spotlighting the one and leaving the other in the dark, and
it is telling that this assessment is used in official circles (2).

I have cited this example of income distribution because
it shows that selective observation is not necessarily good
or bad. It can be defended and attacked on moral grounds.
Relevance is a subjective concept, and if that is already the
case with income distribution, then it is certainly so with
other aspects of reality. Thus someone may be of the opinion that unemployment is of such importance to society
that the diagnosis of the present situation – is the recession
disappearing? – must primarily depend on the development

of unemployment rather than the development of real income. Or, another variant, it may be someone's opinion that 'reality' is governed by environmental pollution and not by the disappointing results of the GNP. My proposition that observation is determined by the observer, and thus by the latter's value judgments, is almost trivial – reality is in the eye of the beholder – except that most economists are only reluctantly prepared to accept it.

And now we have not yet even used metaphors to reinforce the image conjured up by selective observation. Though – those gigantic income recipients – wasn't that a metaphor? And that 'crumbling at the base of the welfare state' – wasn't that a metaphor? Anyone desirous of safeguarding against the compelling effect of unconsciously selective observation must moreover beware of the insidious intrusion of imagery. This point will be taken up in Chapter VIII.

(1)Assar Lindbeck, Interpreting Income Distributions in a Welfare State, The Case of Sweden, *European Economic Review,* May, 1983, p. 227. He places three parades side by side: those of factor incomes, secondary incomes per income recipient and secondary incomes per consumer. The differences between these curves are spectacular. Especially in the case of the last one we see many small persons: almost two thirds of the Swedes are below average. That characterizes the welfare state.

(2)See for instance the *OECD Observer,* March, 1984. It is true that in a verbal commentary by the OECD secretariat the diamond is supplemented by other criteria, including income distribution and the state of the environment. It is also true that the use of the diamond takes place in complete openness, so that everyone can apply his own corrections to it. But it remains a significant case of selective observation in official circles which left-wing observers will find difficult to accept.

Chapter V

# LOGIC

Logic is a splendid thing, and it is quite understandable that some scholars wish to withdraw to this safe ground. Daily reality is rather something for commonplace minds: practitioners of applied economics, journalists, laymen. Or for the brotherhood of econometricians, not commonplace people, but lacking in rigour. The desire to barricade one-self in the fortress of logic is particularly self-evident among those economists who are endowed with a gift for mathematics and high intellectual standards. Economists are very good at deductive reasoning, and especially at its mathematical variants. They have built up a tremendous battery of logical propositions, on which there is a consen-sus – a consensus in the sense that the conclusions have been correctly derived from the premises. In a Walrasian equilibrium system all markets are in equilibrium, every-where the marginal rates of transformation are identical with the marginal rates of substitution, nowhere is there in-voluntary unemployment, foreign trade follows the com-parative advantages, prices are crammed with information and Gerard Debreu is awarded the Nobel prize. Even bet-ter is the simple rule that under conditions of balanced growth the growth of productivity is equal to technical pro-gress divided by labour's share – I seriously mean the latter value judgment – and that the rate of saving has no influence on the balanced growth rate, because the capital coefficient compensates for this influence, after a traverse. The path of growth that maximizes consumption is located where the growth rate is identical with the interest rate.

Unfortunately, the same economic logic also brings us to other possible worlds. An uncorrected disturbance of equilibrium on one market leads to a disturbance on all other markets. In that case all prices contain false information. Incomes are lower than they could have been. Total expenditure does not tally with productive capacity. Either inflation or involuntary unemployment prevails. The system is uncoordinated. A departure from the equilibrium path of growth leads to cumulative disturbances of equilibrium. People pass on the shrinkage in income to one another. In other words, an income multiplier is operative here. Moreover, wealth is affected, and the debtors pass their distress on to the creditors. Here a wealth multiplier is at work. This will assume gigantic proportions if large institutions go bankrupt: insurance companies, banks. If desired, logic points in the direction of a collapse of an international nature. Mexico, Brazil, Argentina are the real-world phenomena that inspire this scenario of financial doom and downfall.

A particularly fertile terrain for deductive reasoning is laid open if we assume that people – subjects, actors, players – react to their environment and to each other. It started in economics with duopoly (à la Cournot, à la Stackelberg), it spread across oligopoly, the theory of games, the behaviour of buyers and sellers in unbalanced markets with various forms of quantity rationing, and suddenly the whole of information science joined in: learning behaviour, search, every possible type of expectation; and in particular the interaction of the one strategic player with the other. For clever minds like Robert Lucas's a world opens in which they can design models and derive propositions to their heart's content. These propositions say little or nothing about the real world; one of the baffling questions is how the jump can be made from logic to empirical statements. But it is indisputable that economists are champion long-jumpers, in any direction.

A horror story of cumulative disturbance of equilibrium is evoked by the logic of environmental pollution. Since Forrester and Meadows we know that we can model the world's downfall: flows, such as agricultural and industrial production, are made dependent on stocks, such as the pollution of the oceans. This dependence is curvilinear; if certain limits are exceeded, nature's capacity for self-purification changes to its disadvantage. The computer helps us to depict the alarming consequences of such relationships. The computer output raises the frightening question whether mankind will make the twenty-first century. But by changing the parameters of the model to some extent, and assuming that people learn from small disasters how to avoid big disasters, the result improves quite considerably.

This brief summary tells us what we already knew, namely that pure reasoning may take us to very different places, just like the railways. As long as the train remains on the rails, we are not guilty of false reasoning. But the terminus-

es differ: Moscow, Madrid, Copenhagen. Where we get
out, that is to say which logical pronouncements corres-
pond to reality, is the central question of economic science.
This comes up for discussion, but the question now is
whether purely logical disputes also exist among economists. These are debates in which the one participant considers the other guilty of false reasoning. Such disputes do
exist, but they are thin on the ground. I shall mention three
instances.

There is in the first place the heated discussion on the
question whether the marginal productivity theory can be
applied macro-economically. A familiar reasoning states
that the interest rate is the derivative from the production
function to the stock of capital goods. Joan Robinson has
called this a harmful swindle. Her argument was that the
value of a stock of heterogeneous capital goods can be
found only by capitalization of a future income flow, and
that calculation presupposes a given interest rate. In that
case the interest rate may not be explained by a function
in which the stock of capital goods occurs as an independent variable. That would be circular and thus false reasoning. The opposite party – notably Paul Samuelson – has in
fact acknowledged defeat. The $K$ from the Cobb–Douglas
function, or from the SMAC, or whatever production function, is a forbidden quantity, unless of course it is assumed
that the stock of capital goods is homogeneous. Anyone so
desirous may assume that, and then the marginal productivity theory becomes a 'parable'. If capital goods are heterogeneous, we fall back on a Walrasian equilibrium concep-
tion to save the marginal productivity theory. Micro-eco-

nomics takes over. For empirical estimates of the stock of capital goods the dispute has little significance, for those are such coarse operations (machines are valued at initial prices, the depreciation is deducted and what is left is artificially inflated with some price index or the other) that theoretical niceties seem rather wasted on them. As a result, this Cambridge–Cambridge discussion is closed for the time being, but it will flare up again sooner or later.

Moreover it leaves a much deeper disagreement wide open. According to a number of Post Keynesians (Sidney Weintraub, Jan Kregel et al.) the marginal productivity theory may not be used if unemployment prevails – that is to say, unemployment on account of a general deficiency of demand. In that situation employment depends on production on the one hand and constant productivity on the other. The elasticity of substitution between labour and capital is nil. It is clear that under these conditions no sense at all can be ascribed to the traditional micro-economic picture of an entrepreneur who tries to maximize his profit by engaging additional amounts of factors of production, until the marginal productivities reflect the factor prices. The neo-classical distribution theory collapses. It has to be replaced by something else – it is still not clear what exactly that is according to the Post Keynesians. An institutional theory about wage determination? A monetary theory about interest? A theory about the degree of monopoly à la Kalecki? Or a tautology à la Kaldor, in which labour's share in national income is determined by the propensity to invest in national income and the two propensities to save of workers and capitalists?

In my opinion the rejection of the marginal productivity theory by the Post Keynesians is based on the assumption that there is no substitution between labour and capital, at least not in a deficiency of demand situation. It is a clay–clay world. That logic is indeed impeccable, but it is of course an open question whether reality looks like that. It seems extremely improbable, and it would in any case have to be investigated empirically, but non-substitutability seems an exception. I have the feeling that the Post Keynesians do not recognize this empirical referee. They try to prove by severe, unshakable logic that in a Keynesian world fixed coefficients exist, but that logic is not convincing. I do not see why positive marginal productivities cannot exist in a situation of underutilized capacity. In that case the marginal productivity theory of distribution is saved. But that does not mean to say that power factors cannot be operative; everyone knows that unions exist that exert influence on money wages and entrepreneurs who try to maintain a certain profit margin. If anywhere, it is here that the possibility exists of a synthesis between Keynesian and neo-classical reasoning. The Post Keynesians will not hear of such a synthesis – which is a pity, because for the rest it is such a likable school. I shall come back to this in Chapter XIII.

A related dispute of a strictly logical nature is Don Patinkin's attack on the Great Dichotomy. It is not permissible to determine relative prices via a system of supply and demand on submarkets and then to determine the price level separately via the quantity theory or a similar macro-approach. This leads to overdetermination in the sense of conflicting equations. Patinkin won this battle, although the empirical significance of his victory remains dubious. The textbooks continue to discuss relative prices and the price level in separate chapters. Theoretical purists, such as Richard Clower and Axel Leijonhufvud, do not commit the sin of the Great Dichotomy, but jettison macro-economics. However, that does not please most economists either.

The underlying question is connected, of course, with the uneasy relation between the micro-economists (who from of old had a leaning towards Walras but are now also alive to a general disequilibrium on all markets) and the macro-economists, who have dominated the field between the Thirties and the Seventies. Most of the contemporary micro and macro observers agree almost unanimously that their systems work out unbalanced, but the approaches are different. The macro-economists think in terms of incomes and expenditure, the micro-economists in terms of wrong signals, disappointed expectations, and a shrinking income passed on from individual to individual. An unresolved question of a logical nature is to what extent these approaches fit together or supplement each other. A question for connoisseurs (1).

While this logical debate hangs in the air (it does not over-excite most economists) I should like to indicate a third point of contention, likewise of a logical nature, and likewise concerning the micro-macro relation, which is of great practical importance. The debate is barely conducted among professionals. It is a dispute between economists and 'laymen'. I do not like the latter expression, but it is unavoidable here, for it is they who are guilty of the false reasoning meant here. Moreover, this false reasoning leads to incorrect actions. The sins against logic are not innocent ones. For the 'laymen' in question are union leaders who create wage inflation, pressure groups who want to have subsidies for everything that's going and conservative politicians who recommend economy and restriction in a depression.

Their mistake is that they generalize from daily micro-experience – sometimes praised as real life, close to living people – towards macro-economics. What in the individual situation is iron logic is known as the Fallacy of Composition for a country as a whole. Economists are aware of this pitfall, but they sometimes forget it under the pressure of with-it, anti-intellectualistic trends. There have always been conservative businessmen who felt that their experience was a guarantee of sound reasoning about the body politic. There have always been people who believed in the warm humanity of the living experience between real men, women and children in the districts and the neighbourhoods, and who then believed that the whole world would behave just like the parts. But that is not so.

Take the following example of iron micro-reasoning. Someone with a money income, irrespective of where it comes from, takes the money to a shop, encounters given prices there, and buys a packet of goods. If income works out higher, real income works out higher. If prices work out higher, the opposite is the case. This order of reasoning, against which nothing can be said, is reversed in macro-economics. A country's real income is equal to the production $Q$. Here too money income $Y = PQ$, and therefore also $Q = Y/P$, but it is not so that an increase in $Y$ leads to an increase in $Q$ or that an increase in $P$ leads to a reduction of $Q$. In the first instance $Q$ is given, and from it the quotient of $Y$ and $P$ follows. In other words, the national product can be sold and earned at all possible levels of money income and the corresponding prices, but the quotient of these levels is fixed if production is fixed. A simple truth, but one which is forgotten again and again.

The forgetfulness occurs among unions which believe that the workers in a country, who already receive the lion's share of national income, can buy more goods as a result of substantial nominal wage increases. Or conversely, in the case of a contraction of real income in a depression some believe that the process can be halted by obstinacy in the wage negotiations.

The forgetfulness also occurs among conservative politicians who believe that a gradual rise in $P$ means a deadly threat to prosperity; inflation must be combated with a tight money policy. The combination of both views leads to continued wage inflation and monetary retaliation – a combination that is extremely bad for everyone's real income. In this way stagflation is promoted, and shrinkflation may be the result of it. It is this enumeration of fallacies that we, as economists, should combat. On logical grounds, but with a view to the political consequences. These consequences have manifested themselves above all in the United Kingdom, and it is therefore no wonder that concerned British economists, such as James Meade, Frank Hahn and Amartya Sen, warn against the policies that are based on a short-sighted *Falsches Bewusstsein*. It is going too far to regard stagflation as a consequence of false reasoning, but wrong thinking does encourage this state of affairs (2).

There is incidentally a second variant of the Fallacy of Composition, which is likewise politically dangerous. This goes as follows. In living reality there is a leaden law that says: more of one means less of the other. That is a consequence of a given income. Even for very rich people more consumption means a sacrifice in the form of less saving. It is tempting, but less correct, to apply this rule to a country as a whole. *'More consumption means less investment.' 'Too low a level of investment points to too high consumption.'* The propositions in italics are correct when the productive capacity of a country is used almost completely, but not in the case of underspending. In that Keynesian situation the opposite may even be true: investments in capital goods suffer when sales are too low, and this situation is summoned up by too low a level of consumption. More consumption can then lead to more capital goods. Anyone who will not see this possibility is making a logical mistake. And once again the logical error is not an innocent one but may lead to a policy of restriction on spending that aggravates the depression. It is not for nothing that the conservative views on overconsumption are often accompanied by mistrust of macro-economics in general and Keynesian ideas in particular. The incorrect logic makes people ripe for a relapse into pre-Keynesian ideas. The concoction is a harmful one, especially if it assumes the form of the sophisticated modernism known as Ratex (see Chapter XIII).

These tirades may sound rather bitter, but they have a hopeful undertone. Economists have at their disposal a logic which in some respects is better than that of people who are close to the so-called warm reality of so-called real life. By this logic I do not mean so much that we can design models with five hundred equations, or that we can prove the existence of Walrasian equilibrium. I mean rather that economists possess a kind of common sense that manages to avoid popular misunderstandings about macro-economic relations. It is not so much to be proud of, but perhaps something. And we should definitely defend this part of the mainstream against the dogmatic attacks from left and right (3).

(1)See the excellent book by E. Roy Weintraub, *Microfoundations, the Compatibility of Microeconomics and Macroeconomics,* Cambridge, 1979. He concludes that modern equilibrium analysis has gone far beyond Walras; it considers transaction structures, information costs, speculation, imperfect adjustment, and search behaviour. This brings it nearer to macroeconomic concerns. What is now called for, says Weintraub, is 'tolerance on the part of economists of all persuasions' (p. 160). And: 'one may guess that eclecticism will be the rule in the near future' (p. 161–162). This conciliatory tone, which I should like to subscribe to, is not heard from the rational expectations school; they are the most aggressive participants in the debate. See for instance the bellicose contribution by Mark H. Willis, 'Rational Expectations as a Counterrevolution', in Daniel Bell and Irving Kristol, *The Crisis in Economic Theory,* New York, 1981. To be discussed in Chapter XIII.
(2)Meade, Hahn and Sen express their concern in *The U.S.A. and the World Economy,* Interviews with A. Heertje, San Francisco, 1984.
(3)After completing the manuscript I realized that logical disagreements are contained in the question of dynamic stock adjustment. That brings the number of these quarrels to four, which still isn't many. What is involved is the iron law which says that flows lead to changes in stocks; per period the books must balance. Anyone who constructs an equilibrium in

the flows and neglects what happens to the stocks may be guilty of false reasoning if the stocks are not in equilibrium at the end of the period. This neglect is blamed on the IS-LM model. This model suggests that interest, national income and investments are determined while in the interim the quantity of money, the quantity of bonds and the stock of capital seek a new equilibrium. The suggestion is contrary to the basic rules of book-keeping. The first authors to draw attention to this stock adjustment dynamics were D.J. Ott and A. Ott, Budget Balance and Equilibrium Income, *Journal of Finance,* March, 1965, and since then C.F. Christ, A.S. Blinder and R.M. Solow, and W.H. Branson and R.L. Teigen have concerned themselves with the issue. The contradiction can be done away with by modelling the movement of the stocks, but that leads to a jungle of complex possibilities in which the attractive simplicity of the IS-LM model is lost. An elegant suggestion for simplifying these relationships within a consistent accounting framework has been made by Wynne Godley and Ken Coutts (Cambridge) in an as yet unpublished article *(Some proposals for the simplification and reorganization of micro-economic theory)*. This is an encouraging example of a synthesis that resolves disagreements.

Chapter VI

## EMPIRICAL STATEMENTS

Here we are at the heart of economic science. That is to say, the genuine theory, which combines logic with empirical research. That is econometrics, the great referee. Logic creates potential worlds without number, but what does the real world look like? Which hypotheses endure for the time being, and which have to be rejected? Which relations between economic variables are currently on hand? And, above all, what degree of influence occurs, numerically speaking? What is economically important in this world in which we happen to live? How do we replace the Greek alphabet by numbers?

Before someone cries 'we know nothing about that, the parameters are unreliable, the structures are soft and economists bicker', the following may be recalled. In 1948 an airlift was organized to Berlin, to supply that beleaguered city. It was an efficient operation, utilizing a new technique devised by G.B. Dantzig, T.C. Koopmans et al.: activity analysis on the basis of linear algebra. This mathematical method can evidently be applied to economic situations to understand them and control them. Admittedly, activity analysis is applied only to parts of reality that are firmly constructed. They are above all production processes with boundary conditions, within which optima may be sought.

In other words, engineering work. In macro-economics relations are, of course, much less favourable; a country is not an airlift. But nevertheless Koopmans was awarded the Nobel prize for work in a general economic field – the methodology of business cycle research – and not only for the intellectual support of logistic operations. `

Estimation of the parameters began with the price elasticities of demand. Since H.L. Moore and H.L. Schultz we assume that these parameters are usually below one. That they have a negative sign is something that we knew even without research (apart from the minor exceptions à la Giffen to which we devote so much attention because they demonstrate the usefulness of indifference curves – the only use that those things have). Respectable studies exist on Engel curves. Macro-consumption equations are alive and well. Recent research by David Hendry et al. has led to a certain degree of satisfaction among econometricians (1).

We cannot, of course, say that of the investment equation. Since Tinbergen pointed to profit as the principal variable in the Thirties, and cast doubt on the accelerator, a long series of researchers have been engaged in understanding investment behaviour, but the success is not overwhelming. One of the reasons is that profits are so difficult to get a grip on. Next, we are concerned not with current profits, but with expected profits, and there the uncertainty enters, the expectations, the psychological mood. Moreover, the ratio between capital resources and indebtedness plays a part – if this has become bad through the depression, capital investments are halted. It is known that the investment equation is the weakest link in our empirical

knowledge, and that this ignorance has serious consequences. For a number of moot points between the schools,
and especially the controversies between the Keynesians
and the monetarists, have the investment function as the
sticking point. If investments react strongly to sales and
weakly to interest the Keynesians are right; in the opposite
case the monetarists are right. That is of practical importance, because in the former case a budgetary deficit is a
good means of getting out of the depression, and in the latter case it is not. We shall come back to this burning question.

Unfortunately, there are more of these uncertain relations, with notoriously weak parameters. These relate to
the supply of labour. We know very well, through introspection, what kind of incentives make people tick, but
their relative strength is the subject of controversy. The
wage elasticities of the supply of male adults are probably
positive and small, but if we take instead of wages the
difference between wages and social benefit doubt creeps in
– some researchers from Leiden and Wisconsin (2) find
substantial values, with as an emotionally laden conclusion
the idea that the level of the benefits has an inhibiting effect, in both the Netherlands and the U.S.A. If we can believe their research results, there is too much 'generosity'
and 'leniency'. Little can be said for certain about the wage
elasticity of the supply of female labour, since this variable
is deluged with quite different factors than wages, such as
the changed views about working outside the home. And
finally wage differentials play an unclear role in training,
despite all human capital models.

It is therefore no coincidence that it is precisely the supply-siders who function as critics of the traditional demand-side macro-economics (the economic system as a well-supervised water supply). In itself nobody can object to incorporation of the supply side – since Adam Smith economists have done nothing else. To the best of my knowledge not a single living economist exists who is right in the head and who denies the overwhelming importance of the productive incentives for work, for investment, for saving. The debate with the Keynesians is therefore not concerned with the sign of these incentives, but with the value of the parameters in question in relation to the value of the parameters operating on the demand side. In other words, the controversy relates to the numbers that have to be filled in. Here only one type of referee can take action, and that is the econometrician. He bears the Popperian responsibility: hypotheses have to be specified and verified.

But the subculture of the econometricians has its own difficulties. One of them is that the same data base can sometimes be explained by rival theories. In that case there is little to be rejected. That awkward situation occurs with production functions. Cobb–Douglas, SMAC and Translog produce a more or less identical fit. As a result, the strategic question of the substitution elasticity between factors of production remains unelucidated. That is not pleasant, for this elasticity plays a part in the theory of factor shares. If its absolute value is less than one, an increasing capital intensity brings about an increasing share of labour and vice versa (Hicks's Law). The estimates of this elasticity, according to a joker, have contracted to a width varying from nearly zero to nearly infinite. It's not as bad as that, but they do lie on both sides of minus one (3).

Another example of material that can be explained by different hypotheses concerns personal income distribution. Both the Pareto distribution and the lognormal distribution (Gibrat) are said to work well, but these hypotheses have a different theoretical background. Pareto distributions suggest to us that society is organized as a kind of bureaucracy, in which people are paid in accordance with the number of their subordinates; the lognormal distribution directs our thoughts towards a skew probability game, in which normally distributed human talents perhaps exert a multiplicative influence on income: society as a game of chance. This branch of research has incidentally become less fashionable lately, perhaps too because the actual distribution differs too much from the Pareto or Gibrat distribution.

More important than these subfields is the matter of the big models. Since Tinbergen gave the impetus to model-building in the Thirties, this art has been practised by many people in the profession. Until the Seventies the mood was approximately that, though the equations were imperfect, one could learn from every failure – usually in the sense that the equations were expanded by new variables, and that new equations were added. Every form of criticism was welcome and led to new additions to the model. Thus, under the influence of the monetarists, the money sphere was included, together with the capital market, portfolio selection, various kinds of money and near-money. In particular the transmission mechanisms between the capital

sector and the real sector received attention. Next a block
was added depicting the wage-price spiral. Cost inflation
and its influence on profit margins could also be fitted in,
whereby the question arose where the ultimate incidence of
strong and repeated cost increases ended up (many suspect
that it is imposed on profits). The production block was refined into a vintage model, in order to give expression to
the influence of wage inflation on the disposal of old machinery. Separate blocks were added for social insurance,
so as to model the endogenous mechanisms of the welfare
state. And public finance was introduced into the system
in different ways, so that in particular the influence of
public deficits on the circulation and the capital market
could be reflected. At the same time various forms of dis-
aggregation took place, for instance for strategic branches
of industry, such as construction, natural gas etc.

These industrious activities of the econometricians led to
growing models, but not to a growing confidence among
economists and the general public. The principal reason
was that in the Seventies there were setbacks in economic
growth and in employment. Although it is in fact ridiculous
to blame the econometricians for stagflation, it did happen.
In Britain in particular many jokes were made about the
negative correlation between the size of the Treasury Model and the growth rate of the GNP. This is the popular
aspect. A better-founded criticism related to the permanence of the parameters; in the Seventies human behaviour
changed, and so did the institutions. The disarray in exchange rates, the oil crisis, the aggressive wage determination and the rapid expansion of social benefit changed not

only the trend of the variables, such as prices, profit margins, investments, growth and employment, but also the economic structure (defined as the form of the model and the numerical value of the parameters).

Such changes in structure are difficult to measure. One of the reasons is that a model can contain a strategic variable that lies low for decades and thus remains unobserved; a quiet, trend-following movement offers the economist little to get his teeth into. A variable of this kind gets too low a regression coefficient. If it then suddenly gets out of step, a violent effect proves to occur. That of course happened with the price of oil, but also with the interest rate. The econometrician is then obliged to tinker with the model. That happened in the Seventies; it means that science is making progress, but at the same time many get the feeling: what are those smart people actually doing with their computers? If at the same time gaps appear in public budgets and unemployment grows, an atmosphere of scepticism, political and intellectual, develops.

However, there are favourable developments to be set against this. It is not generally known that, precisely at a time when some parameters became soft, a new approach based on changeable parameters migrated from the natural sciences to economics. In this method one is interested in the difference between the constant parameters, which are estimated by the method of least squares, and the parameter values that change in the course of time. The latter can be estimated, for instance by the method of the Kalman filters. From the difference between these two series conclusions can be drawn concerning the changes in the behaviour of people and institutions. This new technique, which is known to the subculture of the advanced researchers, has not yet had sufficient opportunity to acquire a clear place in model-building and has certainly not yet led to the disappearance of the despondency that has taken possession of some macro-economists.

And indeed we have to admit that the robustness of the models leaves something to be desired. This is evidenced above all by the fact that we do not know the sign of some reactions. This happens when a variable exerts influence in various ways and those influences are opposites. Two examples come to mind at once. The first concerns the net effect of budgetary deficits on national income. Put in highly simplified terms, two types of reactions are involved: on the one hand the expansive effect on consumption and thus also on investments, and on the other the contractive effect of the deficit, via the capital market, on investments. The first effect has been demonstrated by the Keynesians with their multiplier-accelerator models; the second crowding-out effect is of classical origin. The question is, which effect operates more strongly. This is not known (so that tall tales can be told about it – more about that later). A complicating factor is the time element: it is often assumed that the income-expenditure effects enter into operation somewhat earlier, and the effect on the capital market somewhat later. This makes it difficult for the econometricians to clarify matters. Unanimity on this matter is nowhere to be found, but according to me the neo-classical reasoning is shaky. Listen, you anti-Keynesians.

Let government expenditure, in a situation of underspending, increase by $\Delta G$. Keep the burden of taxation $t$ constant. National income $Y$ will increase via the multiplier $k$ by $\Delta Y = k\Delta G$. Suppose that the entrepreneurs keep their investments at the same level for a time. The budgetary deficit increases by $\Delta(G-T) = \Delta G(1-tk)$. Now private investments react. They are pushed up by the accelerator $\alpha$, so that $I = \alpha k \Delta G$, and they are forced down by crowding-out in accordance with $I = i(1-tk)\Delta G$, where $i$ is the fraction of the budgetary deficit which, via an increase in interest, is charged to investments. The neo-classical effect is victorious as soon as $i(1-tk) > \alpha k$. This is improbable. For $tk$ has a tendency to approach 1; even at a modest value of the multiplier, for instance 1.5, and a marginal burden of taxation of 0.6, $1-tk$ is equal to 0.1. Even if we assume a high $i$ of, say, 0.5, the left-hand term becomes 0.05, a tiny crowding-out effect. The right-hand term will still be 0.15, even at an extremely weak accelerator of 0.1, and that is three times as much. The anti-Keynesians can be proved right only by thinking the multiplier out of existence, which lacks credibility in a situation of underspending, or by setting the accelerator at zero, which means that investments do not react at all to increasing sales. Or they have to deny that such a thing as underspending can exist – which is in fact the line that they take. Or, another possibility, they have to assume that $\Delta G$ summons up a strong wage inflation that smothers the effect on $I$. The latter implies a kind of Phillips curve that neo-classical authors do not wish to hear about.

The above numerical example is not intended to recommend a policy of expanded expenditure. On political grounds every increase in public expenditure and every deficit increase can be vetoed. I am concerned with the analytical side. Subject to econometric proof to the contrary, I remain a Keynesian.

A similar point at issue on the sign of a variable relates to the effect of increases in money wages on employment. Here three views have long been in dispute with each other: money wages hardly have any effect on the real sector, because prices will adjust; money wage increases are good for employment because they increase purchasing power; money wage increases are bad because they cannot be passed on sufficiently in the prices, they reduce profit margins and they harm investments. All three views have had their defenders in the course of time, whereby some nineteenth-century classicists and Keynes were more or less in agreement about the first view, unions defended the second view and the third view made its appearance above all in the Sixties and Seventies. It is difficult to decide who is right in that the positive and negative reactions are governed in strategic fashion by the extent to which the wage increases can be passed on in the prices. The shifting elasticity may be about one, and in that case the traditional Keynesians and the Friedmanians (who are in each other's company here!) are right: nominal wage waves wash through the system, without changing the real quantities much. If the shifting elasticity is low, harm to profit and investment may be expected. We should therefore like the econometricians to estimate the value of this elasticity. They have in fact done so. The result is that this parameter, which differs per industry, is in general low. An OECD study even finds values (e.g. for the U.S.A. between 0.5 short-term and 0.7 long-term) which mean that cost inflation has a destructive effect on the mark-up (4). But we need not assume that this shifting elasticity is constant. It is obvious – a Keynesian idea! – that it depends on the level of expenditure. If that is low, wage increases cannot be properly rolled on. Moreover, the elasticity depends on the size of the cost increases; if the waves of oil price increases, tax increases and wage increases come on top of one another, there is less chance that the market can handle the cost inflation. This occurred in the Seventies, but then it also proved that the elasticity changes. The spiral block of the big models therefore suffers from uncertainty at a crucial point. This can perhaps be eliminated by the new technique, outlined above, in which the econometrician works with parameters changing in the course of time.

Of these two cases in which the sign of the reaction is not certain – the influence of the budgetary deficit and the influence of money wages – the former is worse, because it dominates current politics to a greater extent. Moreover, the budgetary deficit and the resultant growth of the national debt easily give rise to colligation, because 'debt' and 'deficit' are laden concepts, closely connected with fear of bankruptcy. The one opts for stimulation and the other for retrenchment – this choice is governed by faith, hope and charity, but the rationality of the choice requires econometric insight. And that is not yet sufficiently present. (I shall incidentally argue below that the political dispute between expansive Keynesians and the economizers is restricted by pressure of circumstances. See Chapter XI.)

However, the tragedy of econometrics is not exhausted by this. Even if hypotheses have been rejected, by scientific research, they prove not to vanish from the debate. People simply do not listen. The saddest example of this is present-ed by monetarism, and more particularly by Milton Fried-man himself. The monetarists have gained a complete vic-tory over the old Keynesian water supply theory that disregarded money; all modern models contain monetary variables. The transmission mechanisms between the inves-tors with their portfolios and the real sector are being stud-ied. The monetary way of thought has been integrated into the big systems.

But with this synthesis the extreme pretensions of mone-tarism have simultaneously been pricked like balloons. Money plays a part in economic movements, but does not dominate them. All the hypotheses that Friedman has con-structed in the course of time – and which kept on changing – have been rejected. It is not true that the velocity of circu-lation of money is constant; it is not true that the quantity of money is determined exogenously; it is not true that changes in the price level may be ascribed solely to the monetary supply; it is not true that the turning point in the economic cycle is always preceded by changes in the quan-tity of money; nor is it true that people's expectations are so arranged that monetary policy cannot have the slightest effect in the long term. And yet we continue dragging all this around with us, because new extreme adherents turn up again and again. The economic deathblow to this kind of view was administered by the Panel of Academic Con-sultants of the Bank of England. They tested the great work by M. Friedman and A.J. Schwarz: *Monetary Trends in the United States and the United Kingdom: Their Relationship to Income, Prices and Interest Rates, 1867-1975,* Chicago, 1982. Little remains of the view contained in that work. The quantity theory is rejected, certainly for the U.K. (5).

It remains an interesting question why the results of econometric research are sometimes not accepted. One answer is obvious: they are too little known. There is no such thing as a booklet in which the econometric subculture presents a list of the parameter values that have been estimated, together with indications of the degree of reliability and the degree of consensus. I hope that such a list will be produced one day, with an annual supplement. But even if the econometricians find things that are worthwhile, even then the knowledge will in some cases have difficulty in penetrating. There are various reasons for this. People have their value judgments, and they readily reject research results that do not tally with them. But cognitive dissonance is not the only thing. The two subcultures – those of the general macro-economists and the econometricians – lie far apart. The econometricians have their own journals, which are not exactly bedside reading. Their technique and cleverness are forbidding and often they hardly bother to present their results to people. My desire for a handy booklet with measured parameters is often taken as a joke, and so it is, or a half-joke, but I do feel the lack of articles entitled: what have we econometricians found that pedestrian economists and economic journalists can profit by?

Conversely, the economists too are not very helpful in

bridging the gap. They formulate theories that are hardly
quantifiable, for instance because they contain variables
that are almost immeasurable, such as psychological quantities: ex ante investments, the unexpected part of an increase in the money supply. Sometimes this is done deliberately, to make measurement impossible. We see the latter
among hyper-Austrians and among those desirous of tor-
pedoing macro-economics under the motto that structures
do not exist. The latter seems to me highly unproductive
from a scientific point of view. But independently of these
extreme theorists we often see that reflective observers of
society like to tell tales in which the existing econometric
knowledge is not utilized. Even the big textbooks give no
survey of what the econometric colleagues have attained.
Lessening this gap seems to me to be one of the conditions
for deepening the mainstream of economic science.

(1)David F. Hendry, *Econometric Modelling: The 'Consumption Function'
in Retrospect,* paper presented at the European Meeting of the Econometric Society, Pisa, 1983.
(2)This refers to V. Halberstadt, R.H. Haveman, B.L. Wolfe, P.R. de Jong
and K.P. Goudswaard. They have calculated that the labour supply in the
United States and the Netherlands would have been about 10% higher in
1981 if the transfers had remained constant since 1969 *(The Contribution
of Income Transfers to Lagging Economic Performance: the U.S. and the
Netherlands in the 1970's.* Paper for the 39th Congress of the *International
Institute of Public Finance, 1983).* The expressions 'generosity' and 'leniency' are theirs.
(3)E.R. Berndt, Reconciling Alternative Estimates of the Elasticity of
Substitution, *The Review of Economics and Statistics,* 1976, p. 59.
(4)David Encaoua, Paul Geroski and Riel Miller, *Price Dynamics and Industrial Structure: A Theoretical and Econometric Analysis,* OECD working paper, Paris, 1983.
(5)See A.J. Brown, D.F. Hendry and N.R. Ericsson, *Monetary Trends in*

*the U.K.,* Panel Paper n. 22, Bank of England, London, October, 1983. Excellent work on the transactions velocity of circulation of money has also been done by J.S. Cramer, of the University of Amsterdam (The Volume of Transactions and of Payments in the United Kingdom, 1968-1977, *Oxford Economic Papers,* Vol. 33, 1981, p. 234); it emerges that this quantity displays not only a trendwise increase but also fluctuations. In particular, the velocity of bank money appears to be quite variable.

Chapter VII

## VALUE JUDGMENTS

The permanent popular discussion on economic subjects is a collision of value judgments. Do that, don't do that, they (the government) must do this and refrain from doing that. Such statements have little to do with science because they are not falsifiable. Everyone is always right. The debate goes on and on, for people's value judgments differ widely. On faith, on football, on which interests must prevail over others. Like it or not, this debate of the citizens also penetrates the economists' debate, and there a source of confusion arises. What is presented as science is often a barely disguised value judgment. It is economic science that proves that the budgetary deficit must be reduced; that is at least the pretension of some commentators, who would like to see this advice put into practice. In a more subtle sense our observations, and in particular the choice of the relevant observations, are influenced by value judgments. Because logic is a willing instrument, which can take us everywhere (almost), and econometrics is rather unsteady on its pins, the value judgments influence our picture of the world. They penetrate our Gestalt, our language, and in particular our metaphors and our stories. Before we consider the generous facilities that colligation offers us, first something about the economic value judgments themselves.

They come in two types. Some are derived directly from the wallet. We just have to scratch the surface and self-interest becomes visible. Managers consider that managers' remuneration is too low – after all, businesses can't find qualified people for top jobs. Miners consider miners' incomes too low; they can't manage on them. Farmers consider that they are badly done to by the EEC. The American automobile industry considers imports of Japanese cars too high. The American steel industry considers imports of certain kinds of steel wrong. The United Kingdom considers it unreasonable that some countries pay much more to the EEC than they get back. The chemical industry considers environmental legislation too oppressive. The list is long. It is a political diary that appears in the paper every day and keeps alive the idea of wrangling about economic matters. According to Marxist observers, the list of value judgments coincides with the list of disagreements: all bourgeois 'theories' proceed from self-interest. That is an interesting hypothesis which can quite definitely be tested. I suspect that it is not correct.

Because a second type of value judgment exists, in which self-interest does not play an obvious role: the more or less free-floating ideologies. They leave the mind free to roam in any direction. Not only that the highly-paid consider that they could easily earn less – that is a fairly frequent occurrence – and that Galbraith prefers an increased public sector, but normative ideas are sometimes unpredictable in the sense that they would be difficult to think up if they didn't exist. Working on Saturday, or on Sunday, is bad.

An entrepreneur is at bottom bad, an entrepreneur is of a high moral level because he gives (George Gilder), the State is bad in every respect because it is a product of the ruling classes, government measures are good because they are a product of democracy, income distribution that proceeds from the market is in essence just because it reflects productive contributions, income distribution that proceeds from the market is bad because it reflects capitalism, paid labour is good for you, paid labour is bad for you, women are unfit for responsible work, environmental activists are unpleasant, wrongheaded people.

The last idea is encountered among people who do not have the slightest interest in continued pollution of the environment – on the contrary, if there were ever a contradiction between interest and ideology, it is to be found in the dislike and even hatred that the environmental movement apparently generates among otherwise rather sensible people (1).

The ideological values can be systematized. If we leave radical Marxism out of consideration and confine ourselves to the ideologies that accept the mixed economy, three main issues stand out. They relate to income distribution, the position of the individual versus the community, and the future of the natural environment. The issues are not independent of each other; cross-connections and clusters of relations exist. Anyone desirous of discussing them must write a separate book and make allowance for the underlying flows of ideas: Catholicism, Protestantism, humanism. My intentions are somewhat more modest: three well-known standpoints are touched upon in order to indicate the differences to which they can give rise in the selection of relevant facts.

(i) There are broadly speaking three normative attitudes towards income distribution. Egalitarianism considers that everybody's income should be as nearly as possible identical; differences are permitted if there is a good reason for them, and that is usually connected with wants (size of family). Solidarism considers that incomes are quite entitled to differ, provided that it is ensured that nobody falls below a certain level, and strong shoulders must bear heavier burdens. Elitism considers it just and not merely practical that performance is rewarded and excellent performance rewarded in an excellent way.

Most economists are aware of the one-sidedness of pronounced egalitarianism and elitism. They try to adhere to moderate, reasonable views, a synthesis between the viewpoints. But at critical moments reasonable people who prefer not to excite themselves have nevertheless to choose. The moment of truth occurs when the differences at the bottom become greater and social benefit is cut back. Such a development makes much more impression on the one than on the other. Anyone desirous of describing the situation at the beginning of the Eighties can pass this delevelling by, for there are more important things to report; one can also be fascinated by it. Anyone wishing to pass over it can point out that social benefit is still at a high level, and that the real income of the recipients of benefit in Western Europe is higher than in 1970. All this is true. But is it also relevant? That's a matter of taste. It can also be remarked that these incomes are higher than in 1930. It is perhaps an interesting test case to ask which base year is still regarded as relevant.

These three normative points of view can be supported by selective observation, in which good use can be made of the three graphical representations of income distribution. In particular the parade of income recipients yields excellent examples of which we can make good use: giants for the critics of the Super-Rich, dwarfs for the supporters of solidarity, a large mass of more or less modal people for those who claim that equalization has made considerable progress. The latter idea can also be supported by the Lorenz curve: take the average income of the top ten percent and compare it with the average income, preferably after tax. We then find a modest ratio – in the Netherlands three to one – and forget that the spectacular inequality is to be found within the top ten percent.

(ii) Individualism versus collectivism. Economists have an individualistic tradition, climaxing in Austrian School thinking. The individual chooses, and is hampered in his or her choice only by the restriction of income and by nonzero prices. The choice, described by equality of price ratios and marginal rates of substitution, yields an optimum. With an obstinacy worthy of a better cause, this is called rational behaviour. Some neo-Austrians have drawn far-reaching conclusions from this tautology – to such an extent that one may speak of rather ridiculous fallacies. Here is a Nobel prize-winner speaking. Discussing America of the Eighties he says: 'And of course our society is rational,

being constituted as it is of some 230 million utility-maxi-
mizing individuals' (George Stigler, *Economists and Public
Policy,* American Enterprise Institute, Washington, 1982).
Did he count the people in prison, the drug addicts, the
ideological fanatics, the downhearted, the street gangs, the
I-couldn't-care-less brigade, the people who have bought
far too much on credit, the desperate? Are the bankers who
made the loans to Argentina included in the 230 million?
Is the Nobel prize-winner testifying here to an observation,
or to a praiseworthy faith in the goodness of man? In my
opinion he has allowed himself to be overcome by the Austrian point of departure. That point of departure is methodological and entails: 'what people choose is up to them;
we economists do not pass judgment on it, for us eating a
banana is the same as taking a shot of heroin, we leave the
value judgment to the doctor, the parson, the priest and the
judge'. This normative abstention is legitimate but of
course may never lead to the conclusion that what human
beings do always entails a 'rational choice' and even less to
the conclusion: 'society is rational'. A lifetime of practice
with the tautologies of micro-economics can tempt a scholar into strange statements. (And then the same scholar
complains that governments and politicians listen so badly
to economists. He gives all kinds of explanations for this,
but overlooks the fact that some economists assert things
to which one ought to turn a deaf ear (2).)

Individualism as a value judgment means that people
should be allowed to choose for themselves, until the contrary is proved – killing your next-door neighbour exceeds
the tolerance of most individualists. Collectivism proceeds

from something else, namely that people live in social relationships, and their wants and behaviour thus come about in a social environment. The 'acts of choice' are influenced by parents, children, school, peer groups, parson, priest, colleagues, spouse, employer and so forth. Usually there is little to 'choose', and the expression is misleading. This is an observation, and not a value judgment. It is, however, a piece of methodological advice: approach people as social beings. Most economists prefer not to follow this advice – they fear that in this way they will be transformed into sociologists. In my personal opinion that would not be the end of the world; perhaps they would then be less inclined to speak of 'free to choose', 'rational behaviour' and such misleading expressions (3).

However, I am concerned here not with the question whether the dividing line with sociology has to be respected, but with the value judgment that proceeds from anti-individualism. Anyone who recognizes that human behaviour is subject to strong social influence adopts a position that easily leads to ethical statements. However, these are ambivalent. The anti-individualists split into two inimical groups.

For on the one hand the social environment may be regarded as warm, supportive, stabilizing: the small group, the family, the moral peer groups. This positive attitude then leads to rejection of the metropolis with its fleeting, impersonal contacts, and of the distant State with its large, cold bureaucracies. Some economists take that line (4). Conversely, the warmth of the nest may have something suffocating about it: children become the victims of their parents, of the school and of the church. It is the State's task to create as much freedom as possible and, to mention just one example, to give young people of sixteen years an entitlement to income and accommodation. If they run away from home, a subsidized institution takes them in and the State provides subsidized legal aid.

This normative ambivalence is also to be found among those who assume that people are greatly influenced by outside contacts, fairly anonymous ones, preferably in a large, modern city. The metropolis is a crossroads of cultures. Most adherents of individualism regard this as something rather fine: the chance of development is pleasingly great in a pluriform modern society. There is a wealth of information, a differentiated labour market, an elastic credit system; you can become an entrepreneur, practise a liberal profession, enter into the service of a small business or a multinational or a government office. The latter two organizations in particular offer considerable career possibilities. They further individual freedom.

This normative argument can be effortlessly turned upside down. Some individualists and adherents of collective nest warmth regard society as a deadly threat, with its abundance of professional information, its inhuman modern technology, its experts crushing ordinary people, its advertising, its concrete jungles, its doctors (who make people sick), its schoolteachers (who make children stupid), its welfare workers (who make people dependent), its lawyers, and above all its bureaucracies and multinationals. People are not free. They are slaves of their environment, their artificially nurtured wants, the overpowering advertising, the experts. They are one-dimensional.

What do we find? We are intellectually free to 'choose' our own value judgment. We can follow Hayek, Stigler, Friedman, Becker and the other individualists (close acquaintances of most economists), or Herbert Marcuse, Ivan Illich and Hans Achterhuis (not very popular with most economists). We can follow Weber, Mannheim and the social democrats, who regard the State as a benevolent organization – and that comes natural to some economists (to me, too), for haven't they learnt that the State maximizes the welfare function à la Bergson? Or we can follow Downs, Buchanan and Friedman, who see the State as a collection of selfish office-managers, maximizing their own utilities, afflicted with a permanent craving for expansion. We may exclaim as we will, and there is little to falsify. The observed facts follow our story.

But we may not say that economists have nothing to do with these debates, for they determine our view of society. And something that we may certainly not do – I am now criticizing the mainstream of economists – we may not opt for methodological individualism, in which we take for granted the wants of individuals, thus following unwittingly in the footsteps of highly prejudiced storytellers, who consider that a production-oriented society with effective remuneration differentials, high technology, strong professionalization and a growing real income is a desirability ensuing from economic science. Such a society is easy to defend, in a normative respect, and perhaps I'm an advocate

*Jan Pen*

of it, but that does not proceed from 'economic theory'. It's the other way round: whole chunks of economic theory follow from our views and value judgments.

The neutral welfare concept, which is a methodological point of departure, leads economists into another temptation. Anyone who says that 'economics does not judge people's preferences' easily follows that by 'and so the State may not do so either'. There is not a single economist who will *consciously* recommend this error in logic. For we all know the concept 'merit wants' – throughout the world governments find that certain goods have to be produced and distributed, even if the individual consumers are not enthusiastic about them. There are such things as compulsory education and subsidized music, theatre, ballet, sport. That is legitimate. Things are even clearer with negative merit wants: heroin and murder are forbidden. Nevertheless, some economists become slightly suspicious if the government subsidizes painters who cannot sell their products, or keeps journals with a limited circulation in existence. Such subsidies *distort allocation*. Of course, if by 'distort' we mean that only the citizens' wants, as expressed on the market, count. But I should like to point out that the State itself is an economic subject with its own preferences. The neutral welfare concept, which we like to apply to individuals because we want to avoid normative statements, must also be applied to the State. Rulers have their own preferences; perhaps they want to follow a vigorous cultural policy. Who are we to criticize that in the name of economics? Citizens are entitled to do so, but science is not. If we do so all the same, we give economics a bad name (5).

(iii) This third set of value judgments, which I regard as the
most important, concerns nature and pollution. In essence
economists view this in exactly the same way as other human beings. The profession offers no protection against the
irresponsible opinion that, though pollution is an unpleasant spin-off of production, against which firm action
should be taken, it is not so important that it should dominate our view of society. Economists are no more far-sight-
ed than others and, in the event of a conflict between employment and environment, will often opt for employment,
certainly against the background of a depression. They will
perhaps hope and trust that treating technology will solve
the problems of pollution. This is a reassuring idea that
sweeps the issue under the carpet.

On the other hand, economists may also be of the opinion that the environment in Europe is already subject to an
intolerable burden, that pollution is impairing our children's heritage, that progressive technology may perhaps
be cleaning up a little here and there, but is making matters
worse at other places, and that therefore radical measures
have to be taken to halt these processes. The allocation
must be drastically shifted. What we need is fewer cars on
the road, fewer 'movements' of all those people by train
and jumbo jet. The ideology of travelling should be drastically revised. People should stay at home, play the flute and
read books. Acid rain must cease to fall, even if that requires dearer electricity, dearer cars, dearer agricultural
produce. The fuss about the competitive position of a
country must be unmasked as a nationalistic argument.
That the whole of society, with built-in growth require-

ments et al., has to be changed is acceptable or even welcome. All these opinions can be formulated to taste, with
different degrees of emotional intensity.

It is also true of this crucial value judgment, as outlined
above, that the actual assessment of the situation, i.e. the
statistical observation, leaves something to be desired. The
poisoned ground and the dying forests have been inadequately quantified. The normative disagreement can run
riot all the more unconfined because the figures are not
clear to everyone. Moreover, economic theory has not yet
succeeded in compiling and testing reliable hypotheses that
could serve as predictions. True, the computer output of
Dennis Meadows, directed in 1971 at the Club of Rome,
formed an extremely threatening scenario, but it was not
a genuine prediction. Logic gives an insufficiently positive
answer on what is going to happen, and the observations
are selective. Here, if anywhere, we have a problem in
which colligation has free play.

Incidentally, with regard to the environment too it is true
to say that economists may pass no value judgments in the
name of science. It happens regularly. Our professional
training entails that we devote attention to the production
of goods and services, to real income and to the resultant
satisfaction of wants. Common parlance calls this 'the
economy'. Against this we have 'the ecology', by way of
antithesis. That is highly misleading. It would be correct if
nature were abundantly present. Certainly, the latter is immediately corrected if it comes up in the debate. Nature is
no longer a free good. That much we know.

But the consequences of the shortage of clean water,

clean air and unpolluted soil are drawn only rarely. These consequences, which proceed from Hennipman's neutral welfare concept and have been drawn by Roefie Hueting, state that nature falls under economic science, that the new scarcity reduces the satisfaction of wants, that more production does not necessarily increase welfare but can very well reduce it, and that we have to revise the concept of economic growth. If we want to continue to understand by it progress in human welfare, the growth of production must in some way or the other be corrected for the negative growth of the environment (6). (Please note, I am speaking of 'must', but in this case we are not concerned with a political standard but a methodological recommendation.)

What is the intention of these reflections on value judgments? Surely above all this: that economists are citizens and, just like other citizens, have opinions about what should be and what should not be. Their normative opinions colour their view of what is relevant, what may be expected, and how the world fits together. They would do well to recognize these value judgments and to systematize them. True, the profession does not prepare for this, but it is useful to embark on a debate on value judgments.

In that way an error can be avoided. For economists differ from other people in that they tend to give their value judgments a semblance of scientific objectivity. That is a matter of rhetoric. It works. That is as it should be, but it imposes on the economist the duty to watch and control his own rhetoric. One rhetorical artifice – inadmissible, but in common use – is to present some preferences as particularly 'economic'. An increase in real income is 'economic', but a more equal income distribution is a 'social goal'. Pollution is 'non-economic'. Support of the arts by government subsidies is 'non-economic' but'cultural'. In this way a difference of opinion between citizens is ascribed to the profession, which suffers harm from it. We get the reputation of barbarians, vulgar bookkeepers, defenders of the chemical industry, partisans of survival of the fittest.

A cautious elitism that puts income distribution to work for productive incentives, a careful individualism that proceeds from free people in a free society, and a qualified preference for production above the natural environment – these are legitimate preferences, but they are no more 'scientific' or 'economic' than egalitarianism, collectivism, cultural policy, or giving priority to woods and whales (introduced here as a metaphor: these natural phenomena are dying out, and demonstrate what will presently happen to the human race if we continue polluting land and sea. I am already engaged in colligation).

(1)A certain aversion to environmental activists (such as the Greens in Germany) occurs among people who endorse the objectives of the environmental movement. This aversion may assume such proportions that the term *Falsches Bewusstsein* imposes itself. The reason for this contradiction lies perhaps in the fact that the environmental movement combines different objectives and ideas: it includes anti-capitalism, and sometimes more than a touch of anti-democracy. Here and there the movement has become associated with violent groups, which seize the opportunity of every outbreak of trouble to 'expose the structures', which amounts to fighting the police, setting cars on fire and smashing windows. That whole package puts people off who do not have themselves the slightest interest in persistent environmental pollution. This case illustrates the proposition that opinion-forming proceeds in a colligative and associative fashion; clusters of preferences exist. It also illustrates the counterproductive character of the violent demonstrations in the vicinity of Frankfurt against the extension of the airport.

(2)George Stigler, *The Economist as Preacher and Other Essays,* Chicago, Oxford, 1982.

(3)I am quite happy to let economists operate with indifference planes and budget constraints and all the resultant algebra, if they at least once in their lives read a book on the reasons and the motives that inspire people to want to possess and use things. As such I recommend Mary Douglas and Baron Isherwood, *The World of Goods, Towards an Anthropology of Consumption,* New York and London, 1979.

(4)George Gilder is an example, though he can hardly be called an economist. This inspired neo-conservative regards the family as the basis of all that is economically good, and the unattached male as the source of evil (*Wealth and Poverty,* New York, 1981).

(5)See F.F. Ridley, The Poverty of Economics and the Conservation of Buildings, in: W.S. Hendon, J.L. Shanahan, I.T.H. Hilhorst and J. van Straalen, *Economics and Historic Preservation* (Akron, 1983). Ridley is a historian with an open eye for the True, the Beautiful and the Good. In this essay he taxes economists with understanding nothing of these things and thinking only in terms of money, return and the quantifiable. Ridley is fundamentally wrong – if the economist takes his own methodology seriously, he should include *all values.* Of course, many economists descend to what Ridley calls the poverty of economics, and that is a blind preference for what finds expression on the market.

(6)R. Hueting, *New Scarcity and Economic Growth,* Amsterdam, New York, Oxford, 1980.

Chapter VIII

## COLLIGATION

If you ask an erudite person 'what makes the compleat economist?', he will remember Izaak Walton and answer that such a craftsman must not only possess a number of technical skills and an expert knowledge of his fishing gear – he must also have a great deal of insight into the life of the fish he intends to catch. Like the angler, the economist must be handy not only with his box of tricks and his mathematical skills – formerly that was differential and integral calculus, then linear algebra, thereafter topology, and soon perhaps differential topology (1) – but must certainly also have a certain knowledge of human affairs. This requirement can be formulated differently: a realistic view of society, knowing what is important, sensing how things work, balanced judgment, a sense of proportion, whatever we call it. The maximum formulation is: wisdom. That entails at least proper observation; correct reasoning; and a realistic choice, whether or not implicit, of the relevant parameters. But all that is not enough. These things must also be woven into a whole or a Gestalt (2). A properly coherent tale must be told. This is called colligation. Without colligation there can be no wisdom.

Colligation is characteristic of the Great Thinkers. Adam Smith told a clear story, with a point, and so did Ricardo, Marx, Keynes, Tinbergen, Hayek, Galbraith and Friedman. Colligation is also in vogue outside economics: Gibbon, Darwin, Spengler, Freud, Ortega, Foucault, Illich. Some of these scholars have incurred Popper's displeasure. Which is understandable, for the tales differ, but falsification is often difficult or impossible. The picture may be distorted and the story rather mendacious without it being possible to demonstrate this. It is precisely the great thinkers who manage to weave their story so well that it comes over convincingly, although some critical listeners have the feeling that they are having their leg pulled.

A further disadvantage of colligation is that small thinkers are tempted for once to tell a tall story themselves, with the result that at the periphery of economics a general atmosphere of blather occurs – something you wouldn't wish on any profession. Sometimes too colligation coincides with demagogy, and that too you wouldn't wish on economics (3). Some professional colleagues are therefore of the opinion that 'storytelling' should be avoided. It is at best journalism, at worst ideology and certainly not science.

What are the reasons why stories are so difficult to falsify? We have already seen a number of them: some observations can be disputed, and this is particularly true of the selection and the relevance of observations. Someone may remark that the only relevant aspect of capitalist society is the exploitation of the working classes, as emerges from the fact that capitalists' incomes are made without working. Profits in particular lend themselves to colligation, and the resultant consumption is highly conspicuous (see a Medi-

terranean yacht harbour with its interesting fleet). Someone else can counter this in all kinds of ways – profits are
relatively limited, they have a useful function – but this selective observation can nevertheless stand its ground. Or
someone may consider that real income is actually the best
indicator of the economic situation of a country, and distribution problems and environmental problems are of subor-
dinate importance. In that case shoulders are shrugged at
poor people living side by side with great luxury, and pollution is made light of. Here a series of unfalsifiable value
judgments is involved. In my opinion it does not testify to
wisdom, but it does happen. On such foolish observations
a foolish story can be built, and even an immoral one.

Moreover, we have already seen that logic is a willing
tool. Anyone taking the class struggle as a point of departure can reason on from there to all social phenomena: the
State, power, town planning, taxes, subsidies, education,
administration of justice, crime, art, culture, sport, and the
fact that refuse is badly collected in poor neighbourhoods.
Not to mention international connections – *dependencia!*
Logic then assumes the highly compelling form of rhetoric:
reasoning things out stubbornly, with fine examples, firm
conviction. Everything falls into place.

For that is a following property of colligation: it relies
on verification. The examples hurry towards us from every
quarter. A good storyteller is like the Pied Piper of Hame-
lin: he pipes, and the facts follow him. Where they go only
the Pied Piper knows. Now for every story it is possible to
give counter-examples, but these can be discarded as irrelevant, untypical or explicable by a special theory (immuniz-

ing strategy). The storyteller refuses to be distracted, and
because the economic world is large and complex, he can
always find examples that support him, even though they
are located in Hongkong. If necessary he invokes W. Euck-
en, and says that he is engaged in *pointerend hervorheben,*
or making a point pointedly.

All this makes it problematic enough in colligation –
though not always impossible – to see who is right. However, the most controversial complication lies in the use of
metaphors. For a metaphor is a figure of speech, in which
someone speaks of something as if it were something different. It is the intention to bring about a shock effect. The
listener is pleasantly struck, or unpleasantly struck, or takes
fright. It is an invitation to a new way of looking at things.
The metaphor is therefore never entirely 'true'; it contains
an element of mendacity, or at least a joke. 'John is an ass'
is *literally* untrue; John is a human being. True, it is implied
that John is stupid and obstinate. That is a moot point, and
perhaps it is not as bad as that, but the use of the metaphor
always entails an uncertain element. It may be a slight exaggeration. It may be irony. It may be poetry. It may be
a fundamentalist notion, referring to the *deeper* things. It
is difficult really to reject such an assertion. Is society a
prison? Yes and no – it sometimes seems so, and sometimes
does not, that depends on the *locus* of the observer – but
anyone wishing to persist in this metaphor (Foucault) is
free to do so. Are individuals guided by an invisible hand?
Yes and no – but this image has served for two centuries
and influences thought on economic equilibrium. That
*equilibrium* is incidentally a metaphor itself.

For it cannot be emphasized strongly enough: economic reasonings are bursting with metaphors, and so is our subconscious. Sometimes a metaphor stays in our mind when all else has been forgotten. I met someone recently who many years ago had attended my lectures on Keynes. He remembered nothing of them, apart from two things. In a depression national income is *frozen*. And: if you want to ride a bicycle up on to the pavement, you have to ensure that the angle at which the kerbstone is taken is wide enough: *at a narrow angle the cyclist falls over*. I asked him if he thought that this was a correct description of reality, and he confirmed it. He believed in Keynes. But he didn't know why. The Keynesian logic had gone but the emotion was still there. That is the trouble with metaphors: they have an effect on the human mind, just like poetry, but it is difficult to say what that effect actually is. In that way tales continue to exist side by side.

The reader has meanwhile realized that storytelling, including metaphors, emotions and all that, summons up objections. Does that mean to say that we must reject this practice? Must economists cast out the tales and the metaphors? That is a matter of a methodological taste, which is discussed in Chapter XII. My answer is: without colligation economics becomes a bald subject; the economist is not a compleat angler. But others (such as Mark Blaug) think differently about this. However, what I recommend in any case is this: economists must be aware of their own metaphors. They must not supersede them and not pretend that thet don't exist. A study of economic metaphors may be useful. A few small suggestions follow (4).

The metaphors can be subdivided into small, clear ones and large ones, relating to the whole economic system. An example of the first category: my friend the Groningen economist Floor Hartog recently said in an interview in a local paper (*Harener Weekblad,* 29 December, 1983; you see, I get my material from all over the place): 'The higher incomes have been gnawed down to the bone'. Anyone of a sensitive nature sees a dreadful picture. Not only bare bones, but also someone or something busy gnawing them – the Inland Revenue, or the unions, but they are really animals. Wolves, perhaps. Wolves hold their head at an angle, their fore-legs sag, they tear the meat off and then they pick at the bones by scraping their canines along them. Or are they rats after all? It does not say here: 'tax inspectors are a horde of rats, with sharp teeth, who tear away the flesh of the taxpayers, and then scrape those sharp teeth along the bones, and the victim just lies there, and of course dies from this attack, and we watch these dreadful happenings, and we do nothing, and that goes on and on, people are swamped by beasts, they grab first one victim, then the next'. That is not what is said, but then again it *is*: by implication. The emotional effect may be substantial.

Is the statement about the incomes gnawed to the bone true in a more sober sense? Probably not. The recipients of high incomes whom I know are not skeleton-like in appearance, even though they have certain worries. Perhaps Hartog's metaphor is not meant so literally – naturally not, someone will say, the idea is that income differentials are too small to encourage effort. Those who do not like metaphors will now cry: *then say that*. All right, but dull statements do not make much impact. The right half of the brain does not participate.

This example shows that a metaphor with at first a small range can nevertheless contain a suggestion to regard the whole of society in a certain way: in this case as prey, defenceless and moribund. Many metaphors have from the start a wide scope. They relate to society as a whole. Their emotional impact may be high or low. Some of them are restful. Others instigate action or violence. The following list does not claim to be exhaustive, but is intended merely to give an impression of the multitudinous nature of the imagery. We may regard society as the following.

1.   A timepiece. It has been so constructed by the creator that it runs by itself. Or: the invisible hand runs the show. Actually, this is the most powerful metaphor ever invented.
2.   A forest. It grows, and the growth rate is identical with the interest rate. It lives. Trees die off and are replaced by others. Pruning and uprooting can help to keep the forest tidy. The metaphor is tranquillizing – until we discover that the forest may also become sick. Acid rain may even kill it.
3.   A battleground. Two armies oppose one another. Everything that happens is dominated by the conflict. All the ideas that emerge among the combatants are influenced by the turmoil of battle. One party is the master for the time being, but the ruling class of capitalists will presently, after the last battle (crash! bang! wallop!), come off second-best.
4.   A prison. The governor lays down the rules and tries to keep the prisoners calm. Everyone is watched (the pan-

opticon). Everything, and in particular the Welfare State, is aimed at reconciling the prisoners with their fate, so that the place remains governable (Foucault).

5.   A building. It has not been completed, it is not perfect, but it is being worked on, in accordance with a plan or a number of plans. There is an architect. It is not always clear who that is – various suggestions are possible.

6.   A ship. It follows a certain course, there are steersmen on the bridge. The ship is threatened by storms – a firm steersman's hand is needed.

7.   A spaceship, with a limited supply of energy on board. If we are careless with it, a state of affairs will occur that is not consistent with life (Boulding).

8.   A play. The actors play parts inspired by their place in society. They play different parts at the same time. Change of parts may occur. This metaphor may seem rather frivolous, but take care: in Greek tragedy the ending is fixed, and it is not a happy one.

9.   A game. The players follow a strategy, guided or not by the minimax. They can form coalitions. The total spoils are given (zero-sum game), or they vary. Growth is a positive-sum game, depression a negative-sum game, and the players who may influence the choice between the two games are not always pleasant; some of them are quite grim.

10.   A water main. Water is pumped into it. Leaks exist. We also see water basins: the flow determines the supply, and the supply determines the flow. The system can be well controlled, with taps. You can make a representation of it in glass (Ecocirc).

11.   A rocking chair. It keeps on being pushed and thus remains in permanent motion. This motion is quite natural. It should be accepted.

12.   An aircraft on automatic pilot, but from time to time the human pilot has to intervene, otherwise things go wrong. There is also something like a take-off to self-sustained growth (W.W. Rostov), but the situation may become precarious. Flying is never entirely safe.

13.   An anthill. Well-programmed little creatures all resembling each other, except that they are subdivided into two types (workers and rulers). The metaphor is used to express impotence. No choice, no freedom.

14.   A mess of badly informed people, groping in the dark, with in addition a badly informed series of government bodies groping in the dark. Chance plays a major role. The greatest power is called Muddle (5). Lesson: do not be surprised if the results are unexpected and unpleasant.

15.   Stupid, badly informed people, sheep really, who sheepishly undergo the effects of the 'progress' in physics, chemistry, in brief technology. And of the multinationals, which see through things.

16.   Lemmings, on their way to the sea, where they will drown. Lesson: resignation, indignation or action programme?

17.   A human being, usually sick. The economists are physicians, with different diagnoses. The patient is given injections. Good scope for cartoonists.

18.   A person in the act of falling from the Empire State Building. As he passes the fifth floor we hear him say: 'so far, so good' (popular among environmentalists).

19.   Musical chairs (6). However the participants run and
shove, a few always remain without a seat. That's a nice
game if you accept the rules, but if fights break out we can
expect frightful things. The metaphor can elucidate inflation and stagflation.
20.   A network. People do not exist. They are nodes in the
structures. The structures think (Foucault). The idea that
individual human beings have an existence of their own is
a misunderstanding, which will soon disappear.
21.   A collection of actors who receive signals and react
meaningfully to them as long as they remain within a corridor – outside, chaos is born (Leijonhufvud).

These twenty-one metaphors are seldom elaborated and
presented as faithful pictures of economic reality. Usually
incidental reference is made to them, by the choice of the
terminology. A metaphor that is used only incidentally
may nevertheless have a high emotional impact. Scholars
desirous of making a study of metaphors must – needless
to say – study the language and the rhetoric. Economists
do not accord this study high priority; within their subculture it is not done to regard their own and other people's
terminology as something other than a collection of well-
defined cool concepts. This view tallies with the economist's self-image: someone who reasons coolly. Metaphors are warm. So is colligation. So is rhetoric.

The question here is what important disagreements proceed from the narrative practice of economics. Some come
to mind immediately, and the strongest example is formed
by the insoluble dispute between the Marxists and the rest.

The Marxists tell a tightly knit story, the believers are always right and their statements can seldom be falsified. Society is in the grip of the class struggle and exploitation, and those phenomena determine all that we observe. Anyone who disagrees with the Marxist narrative does well to take notice of the risk that he may be accused of having a false consciousness – has sincerity is called into question. A debate has little point – the story can be rejected on moral grounds, but that point of view is not willingly and explicitly adopted by economic scientists. That is not to say that those of us who think differently cannot learn anything from the Marxists. On the contrary, I believe that their criticism of bourgeois economics is useful because as a result of it we can identify the colligative element in the mainstream. Samuelson's great textbook seems a culmination of reasonableness, objectivity, realism and you name it – it is a synthetic, eclectic approach, offering something for everybody. But it is based on a view, and that view can be disputed. Marc Linder's *Anti-Samuelson* (New York, 1977) is a Marxist critique, full of improbable colligation, weighed down by deadly seriousness, afflicted by every fault of dogmatic Marxism – but nevertheless an eye-opener for anyone who really wants to understand Samuelson. Page after page, chapter after chapter, is unmasked as an apologia for over-ripe capitalism. Some parts of the criticism, such as those on international trade, even have a certain plausibility. And yet this *Anti-Samuelson* is rarely cited, and no reference is made to it in *Economics, An Introductory Analysis* itself.

Another great controversy relates of course to the story

born of the marriage between ecology and economics: the theory of the New Scarcity. Reference has already been made above to the scenarios of pollution and exhaustion. They offer ample facilities for selective observation, cognitive dissonance and rhetoric. That metaphors play a part in this is obvious. I do not want to consider this matter here; it is too important to be dealt with briefly, and I would be carried along by conflicting feelings, such as *Angst*, irritation at the ease with which industrialists smooth the problem away, and irritation at the apparent delight with which those who share my sentiments predict the world's downfall. Sometimes I think that we have too few ecological data at our disposal to draw sombre conclusions, sometimes I think the opposite. The prospect is moreover overshadowed by the risk of large, mushroom-shaped clouds.

Instead, another debate of a colligative nature: the neo-classicists versus the Keynesians. Economists have more experience with that. The point I want to stress is this: both stories are plausible and perhaps even convincing. This suggests an obvious imperfection in economic theory. Here progress can be made only by quantitative research into the economic structure. That progress requires an eclectic procedure, in which we try to combine the usable elements of both views.

(1)This, dear reader, is irony. How many of my professional colleagues are really familiar with topology? And am I, for that matter?
(2)Gestalt is not the sum of the observations, but more than that. When you listen to a Bach fugue, you hear more than the sum of the notes. Moreover, modern neurology takes the point of view that observations

do not enter via the sense organs, which function as 'doors of perception' – it is the other way round. First and foremost is the nervous system, which is seen as a system controlling both behaviour and perception. The sense organs are instrumental in constructing and updating a map of the outside world. This means that all observations are selective; the nervous system determines what can and will be observed. These ideas are defended by J. Droogleever Fortuyn, On the Neurology of Perception, *Clinical Neurology and Neurosurgery*, Vol. 81-82, 1979, p. 97. According to him Gestalt is still too limited an idea – it is too static, and underestimates the permanent updating of the world. Viewed in this light it is not surprising that different people have a different view of the outside world. Since economists possess nervous systems, this neurological insight perhaps explains something of the controversies.

(3)There are many examples of blather or demagogy. Blather reminds me of Marshall McLuhan's 'the medium is the message' and Michel Foucault's indigestible pap of 'mots et choses', but they are not economists (although Foucault is full of information on what economists think, according to him). George Gilder believes that economists want to eliminate uncertainty, and he considers that a very bad thing. These examples are innocuous compared to the remarkable tract by Lyndon H. LaRouche and David Goldman: *The Ugly Truth about Milton Friedman*, New York, 1980. They try to prove that Friedman is a fascist (for his defence of Hjalmar Schacht), but also that Austrian economics, W.S. Jevons, Alfred Marshall, Wesley Clair Mitchell, Oxford 'Kookonomics', the *National Bureau of Economic Research* and the University of Chicago are all members of one big conspiracy that goes back to Jeremy Bentham, and is directed against America. The crash of 1929 was deliberately caused by the British and by a group of American bankers led by Paul Warburg. Hovering in the background are the Mont Pelerin Society and the Fabian Society. All these threats can be countered by a new economic theory, the LaRouche-Riemann model, in which the 'free energy ratio' plays a central though unclear role. I thought at first that this book was a parody (the British Empire was founded on the opium trade and homosexuality) but that is not so. It is a form of colligation with serious intentions and LaRouche seems to be running for President of the United States.

(4)On metaphors there is an extensive literature which – here follows a hypothesis – is largely unknown to economists. I myself have found valuable sources in J.J.A. Mooy, *A Study of Metaphor*, Amsterdam, 1976, and the collection *Metaphor and Thought* (edited by Andrew Ortony, Cambridge, London, New York, Melbourne, 1979). Constantly recurring

*Jan Pen*

questions are: is a metaphor something that is in fact impermissible in
science, because it gives a false picture? Someone says this and means that
– surely that's unscientific? Or is the metaphor an innocent something, a
decorative element, enlivening rhetoric? Or is it a thing of beauty, stimulating the mind, producing new insights, explaining the world? There was
a time when metaphor was mistrusted, in Locke's footsteps, but recently
a revaluation has been going on. One of the philosophers who has made
a considerable contribution towards that is Max Black (*More About Metaphor* in the above collection). There are of course exceptions to the rule
that economists are not interested in their own metaphors. Kenneth
Boulding is one of them. *The Image, Knowledge in Life and Society,* Ann
Arbor, 1956, is an inspiring book, to which reference is hardly ever made
in recent literature. Boulding advocates the study of imagery as a separate
field: *eiconics,* a metatheory which comprises all the behavioural sciences.
In a later publication (Metaphors and Models in the International System,
in R.J. Akkerman, editor, *Declarations and Principles,* Leiden, 1977),
Boulding draws attention to the contrast between models, which are clearly defined, and metaphors, which are not, and which can have a confusing
effect, certainly on the policy-maker. He argues that recent American foreign policy has suffered greatly from the use of absurd metaphors.
(5)Anthony Sampson, *The Anatomy of Britain,* London, 1962.
(6)Musical chairs and many other metaphors are used by Thomas C.
Schelling, *Micromotives and Macrobehavior,* New York and London,
1978. Schelling shows that metaphors and precision can go hand in hand.

Chapter IX

# TWO PLAUSIBLE STORIES

First story. Society consists of rational actors, who are perpetually choosing and making decisions. They are considering whether they shall eat an additional apple, purchase an extra year of education, erect an oil refinery or go out burgling that night. They are confronted with constraints, principally their own income, which is constantly shifting to the right, and the twenty-four hours of the day. And they receive signals. These are mostly price signals that give expression to scarcity. The individuals engage in transactions and the price vector clears all markets. The invisible hand ensures that everywhere marginal rates of transformation are identical with marginal rates of substitution. Allocation agrees with the well-ordered preferences of the individuals. The most active people become entrepreneurs; other prefer to become employees. The entrepreneurs are busy all the time innovating and investing; in the latter case they are constrained by a given volume of savings that is determined by the time preference of the individuals. Real income per head is fixed by the participation index and by labour productivity: the latter grows with the quotient of technical progress and labour's share in national income. This share is identical with the labour elasticity of production. The growth path is therefore fixed. Individual incomes are determined by marginal productivities and the factor endowments. Risks can be insured against; uncertainties are discounted in the behaviour of the individuals and find expression in the prices. Rational decision-makers entertain rational expectations. It is a well-oiled machine, which works. The past proves that.

Of course, disturbances may occur in the harmonious whole. Market imperfections exist. Prices occasionally react rather sluggishly. Innovation entails creative destruction, and therefore businesses keep on disappearing. But against the contraction at the one place is expansion at the other. Total productive capacity is utilized, on account of Say's Law and the constant urge of individual people to improve their position. A temporary lag in growth may occur, for instance because innovations weaken somewhat, or at the traverse from one growth path to another. The system is flexible, but sometimes too stringent requirements are made of the flexibility – then things go somewhat less well for a while. Recessions occur and – temporarily – depressions. They pass over again. They always have done. There are, of course, also external effects, which have to be internalized via the price system (a task for the government). Market imperfections may have a painful effect regionally, branches of industry may languish, and that is unpleasant. Sometimes excessive investments have to be written off – that may be quite disagreeable to the investors. But these disturbances, whether cyclical or not, are limited and cannot affect the underlying equilibrium-restoring forces.

Unemployment is hardly to be expected. Jobless people do exist, but their situation is a voluntary one. They are looking for a job and the search may take a long time because their requirements are high. They refuse to accept a lower wage at which they can find work. Social security and minimum wages increase this type of leisure. Unemployment fits in with the preferences of the jobless.

The real threats come from outside the market sector. Pressure groups may become too strong, apply restrictive practices, throw sand in the works (Mancur Olson). The money-creating institutions can make inflation and render possible wrong investments (Wicksell, Friedman). The unions can restrain productivity. The greatest threat comes from the government, which regulates too much, places too heavy a burden on economically active people, drives a wedge between the income that people earn and the income that they actually receive, and displaces private investors from the capital market. Pressure groups rummage about in the exchequer and create entitlement programmes. Budgetary discipline is in danger of being lost through the pressure of the Keynesians. Budgetary deficits are defended or promoted. All that happens under the flag of a benevolent regime desirous of rectifying 'market failures' but in fact creating them; desirous of curing 'instabilities' but in fact having a destabilizing effect; desirous of furthering order but establishing bureaucracies; desirous of increasing people's welfare but in fact increasing poverty and dependence. Every slight unevenness in the human course of life is seized upon by false prophets as an excuse for thinking up new rules and imposing new burdens, until the system no longer works. This is the way to slavery.

But fortunately people are rational. Consequently, in a

democratic system they can keep the irrational politicians, money-creators, Keynesians and bureacrats in check. Fortunately it is being increasingly realized how the world is constructed. The prospects are therefore not bad. At a growth rate of three percent real income doubles within twenty-five years. That is the underlying trend.

Second story. Society consists of individuals groping in the dark. They are badly informed, and information is costly. They do not know their own wants, which keep on changing and are strongly influenced by the supply of new products and advertising. Consumers influence one another, in fashionable waves. The price signals that people receive come from oligopolists – these prices are fixed arbitrarily. Only by chance are they equal to the marginal costs, and they say nothing about scarcity. Price determination is in many cases a question of power. Moreover, the price signals are false in times of overspending and underspending, i.e. almost always. These false signals operate systematically in the wrong direction, in the sense that they aggravate overspending and underspending. The markets fail. They do not clear. The system is chaotic and highly instable.

The growth path of production is determined by the investors, who are not constrained in their decisions by the volume of savings – the latter adapts via the multiplier. The investing entrepreneurs are impelled by animal spirits, which in turn are subject to waves of a mass psychological nature. Growth proceeds by fits and starts, partly because technology progresses by fits and starts. Technical development is determined by a vanguard of large businesses, and emulation by others depends on the level of spending – since the latter is unstable, the jerky nature of growth is also accentuated (1). Slow growth easily veers round to negative growth, on account of the accelerator. The system tends constantly towards underspending. Incomes are repeatedly disappointing. The growth rate of production is constantly lower than the growth rate of productivity, and there is a constant tendency to lay off labour. Unemployment grows – only occasionally is this masked by overspending. The labour market is not self-regulating, because the demand is inelastic in respect of the nominal wage, or worse, because too high nominal wage increases, which the unions attend to, further impair employment. Profits are usually too low and unevenly distributed; and a permanent squeeze is going on, which is slightly compensated for only in a situation of overspending. This squeeze is further concealed from view because there are always quick growers with striking profits. These attend to an additional push in certain sectors and contribute to the instability.

In this chaotic whole the government can try to play a stabilizing role. However, this is thwarted by the unions with their wage inflation, the pressure groups that force up government expenditure in a situation of overspending, and the conservative financiers who oppose a budgetary deficit in a depression. The government itself is rather chaotic: all kinds of agencies work at cross-purposes. The Keynesian lessons are put into practice very inadequately. If it does happen, it happens in spite of the ideology of the governments: Reagan allowed the budgetary deficit to in-

*Jan Pen*

crease, and therefore did the opposite of what he had promised. He is a kind of Keynesian (to the sarcastic joy of J.K. Galbraith). But the stagnation cannot be properly overcome in this way, and above all unemployment will continue to grow.

The repercussions in the social sphere of stagnation, inflation and increasing unemployment are enormous – a new class gulf is formed, between those still working and those laid off. The latter become alienated from society. The welfare state cannot be maintained, social benefit is reduced, just at the time when it is most urgently needed. This breakdown leads to further embitterment, drug abuse, hopelessness. Crime increases, but the prisons are overfull. Criminals run wild. The crash of glass is heard in the streets. Western society is passing through a deep crisis (and the crisis in economic science is a reflection of that).

These are two mainly plausible stories, and yet they are opposites. In my opinion we have seized here on the second most important contrast between economists (the most important one relates to pollution). It can perhaps best be labelled as neo-classical versus Post Keynesian.

Which is the more convincing? That is difficult to say. The two views can be backed by a great wealth of observations, anecdotes, metaphors, relating to all possible countries and times. There is ample scope for verification. Falsification, on the contrary, rebounds from the shoulder-shrugging argument that the counter-examples are hardly relevant.

Take for instance the Seventies, in the industrialized

world. What happened there is known. The data are co-pious; they point to stagnation, increasing unemployment, bankruptcies, growing budgetary deficits, a general sense of alarm. The one surprise succeeded the other, and none of them was a pleasant one. The curious fact occurs that these events can be used as proof of both stories. The Keynesians can point to the chaotic nature of the events; the development of production is far below the trend, un-employment is far above it. But, strangely enough, the neo-classical story also has a strong case. We must of course di-vest it of its nonsensical excesses, such as the idea that all unemployment is voluntary, and more generally of its ra-tional expectations basis. In the Seventies we note the un-derlying cybernetics, at least if we are prepared to see them. And then the recent past gives grounds for moderate op-timism.

For the Seventies abounded to such an extent in shocks – the collapse of the Bretton Woods system, the steep rise in oil prices, the accumulation of liquidities among the OPEC countries, the shift in the international division of labour, the violent wage inflation – that we really could have expected a much sharper drop in real income. Keynes-ian theory predicts a depression at the moment when the growth curve bends down. But the system is not that unsta-ble. The oil shock was followed in most countries by a year of zero or negative growth (1975), but over the whole peri-od of the Seventies growth persisted. The trend was some-what lower than the excessively high growth rates of the Sixties, but most countries carried on well (exception: the United Kingdom). True, a hardened Keynesian may argue that governments followed an expansive policy, perhaps in spite of themselves, by allowing the budgetary deficit to rise, and that this absorbed shocks; but the system is more robust than the tall story about instability would have us believe, and the supply shocks explain the stagnation. In the view of a supply-sider, there has hardly been any 'underspending' either; insofar as governments believed that and blew up demand, they simply aroused inflation. The painful question remains: who is in fact right?

Economists may react differently to this ticklish question. A cheap answer is: both stories are exaggerated, the truth lies in the middle. In that way we make no choice, nor do we know whether our world is stable or unstable. A second, more sophisticated answer: these stories are unscientific. They contain a hard core on which judgment may not be passed because it is a consistent system, but they lead to research programmes. These research programmes are fruitful or not – that remains to be seen. The best paradigm leads to the most interesting hypotheses, and it may well be that some hypotheses remain standing after being put to the empirical test, and fairly firm parameters are found. The neo-classical view has led to considerable research, and so has the Keynesian view. In this way our knowledge progresses. Perhaps a synthesis is possible, in a large model.

I sympathize with the idea of a synthesis, but still I regard the latter answer as unsatisfactory. For the conflict between the neo-classical school and the Post Keynesians is not merely a conflict between two research programmes. If that were so, we could encourage the teams to score better in the research field, and perhaps yelling and cheering is a pleasant relaxation in the business of science. But it does not solve our dilemma: how are we to regard the society of today? What kind of times are we in fact living in? Shall we get out of the depression? What must we do, wait and see, stimulate, or what? What party must we vote for? How should we interpret our daily paper? What is in fact our identity?

I am therefore personally inclined to welcome a third answer, which has been suggested by Axel Leijonhufvud (2). The idea is that the system is reasonably stable within certain limits, but not outside them. Leijonhufvud speaks of a corridor (another metaphor). As long as the departures from the neo-classical path of growth are limited, we may expect that the equilibrium-restoring forces maintain the upper hand, and outside the corridor that is not so. In that case the cumulative disturbance gains the upper hand. This view is in a certain sense trivial – it is reminiscent of the diagnosis of the psychologist who says: 'this person is proof against shocks as long as they do not become too great. Under too heavy shocks he is in danger of showing signs of stress'. But we cannot dismiss it like that. Leijonhufvud's suggestion raises the question of the factors that determine the limits of the corridor (3), and above all too whether a country is inside or outside the cybernetic system at a given moment. Can we say that the United Kingdom is now inside or outside the corridor? And France? And Brazil?

It goes without saying that economists should be able to answer such questions. Unfortunately, it also goes without saying that they cannot. The answers with which they come forward – whether or not under compulsion – are born outside science proper. Thus I am personally inclined to the opinion that most Western countries were outside the corridor at the end of the Seventies and the beginning of the Eighties, but that they have been temporarily brought back into the corridor by the massive budgetary deficits, especially in the United States.

However, this does not solve the problem of the coming decades, for an increasing national debt leads to an increasing burden of taxation in the future. That has an inhibiting effect on production, and the danger that we shall presently find ourselves outside the corridor again grows. Worse still, public debts themselves have a destabilizing effect, as soon as mistrust in the debtor's solvency occurs. That is now the case. In my opinion the most dangerous macro-economic development lies in the debts. This development is acquiring a grim dimension through the threatening bankruptcy of Brazil and Argentina. This can lead to chain reactions and collapses in the world of banking, and to a deep depression before which that of 1929 fades (4).

Economists therefore remain at a critical point with a considerable degree of uncertainty. We cannot say that they are empty-handed. On the contrary, their hands are over-full. They have more arguments than they can handle. The choice between the neo-classical and the Post Keynesian story is difficult to make. That, of course, influences our view of politics.

(1) The interaction between technical progress $t$ and the growth rate of production $q$ can be illustrated by the following small model, which stresses the importance of expenditure and tries to synthesize Schumpeter and Keynes. We assume that the growth rate of production is equal to

$q = k.a + t$, in which $k$ is the multiplier and $a$ an autonomous impulse. Now let us assume that $t$ is partly autonomous – the production growth among the front-runners – and depends in part on $q$. The latter is plausible because firms need an expansive market to follow the innovations of the leading group. Thus $t = t_0 + \theta q$, where $t_0$ is the autonomous technical progress and $\theta$ the growth intensity of technology. The consequence is that the growth rate is equal to $[k/(1-\theta)]a + [1/(1-\theta)]t_0$. With a modest multiplier of $k = 3$ and a $\theta$ of 0.5, this gives a Keynes–Schumpeter multiplier of 6. If $a = 1\%$ and $t_0 = 1\%$, the growth rate becomes 8%. But what happens if the spending impulse is negative? It is only a model, the parameters are unknown, time-lags can upset the game – but nevertheless, what instability!

(2)*Information and Coordination, Essays in Macro-economic Theory*, New York, Oxford, 1981.

(3)I have attempted to give a reply to that question in 'On Eclecticism' (*De Economist*, 129, No. 1, 1981). The list of factors determining the limits of the corridor is a long one. The research programme that ought to be directed towards the quantitative determination of these limits is a life's work. Leijonhufvud himself has not started on it.

(4)See W.R. Cline, *International Debt and the Stability of the World Economy*, Cambridge, London, 1983. This is an extremely gloomy story.

Chapter X

# POLICY ADVICE AS SUPERCOLLIGATION

Economists derive their prestige from the self-assurance with which they give policy advice. However, that's a mixed blessing. If things go badly with trade, the economists get the blame. In their turn they try to shift the responsibility to the politicians, who do not follow the recommendations of science, but the politicians defend themselves with the argument that those recommendations are not identical. Economists' disputes seem to be political disputes, and that attracts attention. In the public discussion such disagreements are accentuated – that is a part of democracy, for democracy is a permanent, heated debate, and the temperature increases in times of setbacks. In this way economists get a bad reputation, which is the other side of their prestige. Bill Schorr's cartoon in the *Los Angeles Herald* (1982) sums it up neatly. On a bench is sitting a shabby man, who is saying to his neighbour: 'First I was a Keynesian – next I was a monetarist – then I was a supply-sider – now I am a bum'.

Scientists can withdraw from the political scuffle and the hubris of their politically outspoken colleagues by remarking that these are disputes between citizens in which they have no concern. Science cannot pronounce value judgments and thus cannot give policy advice either. This view, which is entirely correct, is often defended but rarely taken seriously and even more rarely put into practice. Perhaps that is because economists sense that their narratives, which contain no explicit policy advice, are still tainted with value judgments, so that they have already offended against the prescription of falsifiability. In that case one might just as well offend a little further, and attach a political value judgment to the story. This can even go so far that colligation is transformed into ideology – the political intention is in the forefront here, and observation, logic and colligation are subordinated to policy advice, which was fixed in advance. That is regarded as bad because it is dishonest – but it is even worse when people in all sincerity believe absurd things and when these beliefs have disastrous consequences. History, and recent history is no exception, is full of examples of tragic misunderstandings, leading to the relentless pursuit of dubious goals. The class struggle, mistaken suspicions about productivity increases, the idea that strong nominal wage increases will raise the real income of all workers; short-sighted nationalism; fanatical monetarism; right-wing hatred of the welfare state; all these ingredients are clearly discernible in modern society, and economists tell ideological tales based on them. In the name of economic science, this is of course wrong. But if the ideology turns out to be reasonable and convincing, we should be somewhat more tolerant of the economist who confuses economic theory and political advice.

Nevertheless, I believe that we must recognize the methodological sin and combat it wherever it crops up. If an economist suggests that the government must take measure

*A* and not measure *B,* a highly complex judgment is pronounced. In the first place a given situation comes under review, and is put in a colligative context – in many cases that already contains selective observation and a number of value judgments. Then something is assumed about the effect of the advocated measure, and that too is usually a rather complicated tale. Finally, it is posited that the result aimed at improves the existing situation, a proposition about which disagreement is always possible.

The latter is crucial. Every government measure, however well-intended, harms somebody's interest. Pressure groups put it differently. In their rhetoric the public interest is served by a new factory that creates jobs and incomes, and they don't mention the neighbours whose view is spoilt, the harm to other firms and the input of energy and raw materials that does environmental damage. Particularly in the case of government expenditure it is easy to concentrate on the striking benefits and to forget the costs. Benefits and costs almost always accrue to different people. Those people are not identical in income, age, place of residence. Some are as yet unborn. It is the duty of economics to point to these invisible or less visible costs, and perhaps it can indicate the differences between the groups, if any. This does not eliminate the conflict of interests but it brings it out into the open.

Science cannot act as referee here. This goes without saying when obviously conflicting objectives are involved between which science cannot choose. But it is of universal validity. Even an apparently reasonable desire for full employment may be disputed. 'Why that strange work ethic?', someone may counter, and he or she may keep that up in the face of all kinds of admonitions. We are concerned here with a non-falsifiable statement. It therefore seems hardly exaggerated that policy recommendations involve a form of supercolligation and fall entirely outside the field of science. Policy advice is the field of citizens, politicians, civil servants, editors-in-chief, television commentators, everybody. Excluded is only one category of human beings: economic scientists. All the amateurs are competent, the professionals are not.

This paradoxical result may be methodologically correct, it is at the same time unsatisfactory. It seems as if economic science is of no importance to practice. Hardly anybody wants that. If the profession wishes to be worth the trouble, it must be policy-relevant.

The dilemma can be solved in various ways. The pure and chaste solution is that economic science provides information on the way in which the world is constructed and then leaves it to the citizen to draw political conclusions on the basis of that information. The citizen thereby makes the jump from *is* to *ought*, with all the resultant capers – but that is something to which citizens are accustomed. They do nothing else all day long and a part of the night. Economics has to ensure that the is basis for this jump is as sound as possible. That is to say, no exciting descriptions of non-existent worlds, not too many announcements about barely relevant phenomena such as Reswitching, the Standard Commodity, the Walrasian Equilibrium, but relevant information on observable facts and relations. This is a clean solution, which nevertheless is regarded by some fellow-economists as too unproductive and a bit hypocritical.

The next solution, welfare economics, is an alley full of temptations. Not necessarily a blind alley. But welfare economics is positive theory that tries to discover the factors that determine human satisfaction. Human satisfaction, that slippery concept, is taken at face value: people are satisfied by what they choose. Consequently, welfare economics is not a normative theory, despite the view of E.J. Mishan and many others (1). The misunderstanding arises almost automatically, because the central tenet of welfare economics relates to Pareto's *optimum* – the allocation that is 'the best' in the sense that any other allocation yields less satisfaction. 'Well then!', cries someone who hears this for the first time, 'isn't that allocation the best? Dammit all, you ourselves call it optimum!' The answer must be: '*peccavi,* we should never have used the word optimum. For what if the preferences of the economic subjects, which is what it's all about, happen to consist of several shots of heroin a day?' And moreover Pareto's optimum is based on the rule that *more is better* – that too will not be subscribed to by every citizen. In fact welfare economics can furnish a series of useful insights, into price distortions, externalities, charges and subsidies on specific goods, and above all into environmental damage; that may be illuminating for anyone wishing to form a political opinion. It reinforces the is basis – see above – but it does not jump.

The third solution for the relationship between theory and politics is the most interesting one. It is based on the separation between means and ends. The citizens, and

especially the politicians, decide on the ends that they want
to pursue and let the value judgment spread its wings.
Science seeks the matching instruments, and makes statements about the relations between means and ends. These
are falsifiable statements. It seems an attractive, clear separation. This was formalized by Tinbergen (2) and others,
with the aid of the decision model. This separation does indeed prove to be the salvation of science. We may never
give it up, however much we doubt it.

The separation between means and ends works well in
special situations that satisfy strict conditions. The ends
must be recognizable, uncontroversial, and, in the ideal
case, fixed quantitatively. The instruments must be neutral,
that is to say that they must not be loaded politically. These
instruments must preferably be quantifiable. The decision
model must be accepted, with reliable parameters. And,
above all, the whole operation must be performed in a cool
atmosphere, without colligative context. In that case policy
advice is a piece of economic engineering work, and that
is what it is meant to be.

These conditions are best met in the case of logistic problems, such as the efficient use of a fleet of ships and aircraft;
the allocation of funds to various divisions within a concern; the calculation of optimum stocks, including liquidities; the construction of cars and ships. The computer can
assist in this. These techniques have assumed major proportions. All large firms utilize them, and that increases
their productivity.

In the political arena the separation between means and
ends is a good deal more delicate. Here we encounter a

number of complications, some of which are fairly lethal.

1. The objectives are seldom given, and hardly ever in quantitative form. Politicians have a tendency to want everything at once, not to say exactly what they mean, and sometimes flatly to conceal what they have in the back of their minds. In the present times of unemployment many a politician claims to be pursuing the restoration of full employment. But when it comes down to it, they prove to give priority to other objectives, such as free wage negotiations, a lower budgetary deficit, a strong currency, lower price inflation, laissez-faire. The priority of employment is openly avowed, but without exaggerated sincerity.

The answer of the policy-oriented economist to these conflicting attitudes is as follows. In a discourse between politicians and scientists the ends must be explained and enumerated. It is science's task to say to the politicians: 'what you want cannot all be done at the same time, priorities have to be set'. The politicians are forced to make themselves clear. This *aufklaerende* task of the economists leads, however, immediately to new disagreements and petulance. Politicians do not like to hear that they make inconsistent statements – their task is precisely to preserve via such statements sufficient freedom of policy against the rank and file, Parliament, dissidents in their own party. They live by the grace of a certain noise in communication. If opinionated economists put their finger on that, they are informed that they are opinionated economists who belong in the study (and they are moreover informed that economists always disagree with one another). All this contrib-

*Jan Pen*

utes to the profession's bad reputation. We must not derive from it that the debate between politicians and economists on the objectives of policy must be dispensed with; on the contrary, it must be conducted, but its success is limited and the by-product is a strengthening of the view that economists are trouble-makers.

2.   A second complication is that objectives, even if they are clearly presented, cannot be attained if there are too many of them. One of the rules of play of the decision model states that we must have as many instruments as targets. In hard reality the number of targets exceeds that of the instruments. There are two formal solutions for this. The optimistic solution is Tinbergen's: seek new instruments of economic policy, so that the decision model becomes capable of solution again. A familiar example is non-inflationary incomes policy, which has to come to the assistance to combine full employment – which is pursued with budgetary policy – with a more or less stable price level. However, these creative suggestions can come to naught if the number of objectives grows very quickly. And that is exactly what happens in a democratic country. The requirements that people make of their governments are so high in the welfare state (in the fields of income distribution, health care, subsidized housing, subsidized transport, the growth of production necessary for full employment) that they cannot be met. If this is attempted, it leads in turn to an excess of regulation.

  Here we therefore encounter the additional complication that the instruments are rarely neutral. They are always politically charged, as a result of which they are rejected by pressure groups. That happened with wage policy; the government-controlled variety harms the bargaining freedom of the unions, and guidelines are effective only in those cases in which they are adhered to – that consequently creates inequities and injustice. Taxes are not pure instruments either: every tax may be described as a bad tax, from the point of view of those who have to pay it. Every instrument has a target character, as a result of which the number of objectives continues to exceed the number of instruments. Economic engineering loses its 'neutral' character and its effectiveness at the same time.

The pessimistic solution for an excess of objectives is Theil's: the economists must confront the politicians with the excess of good intentions. This fits into an old tradition of economics; we must be aware that more of one means less of another. The exchange must be formulated and quantified as sharply as possible, preferably in the form of a complete cost–benefit analysis. The politicians must then sort it out for themselves. This is in fact a workable solution, though it must be remarked that economists are again in danger of acquiring a bad name. They are now the pessimists who say: 'so you want all those wage increases? OK, but it'll be at the expense of employment, and soon at the expense of real income'. Or the economic adviser says: 'you want a tight money policy to combat inflation? OK, but it'll be at the expense of employment and real income'. The emphasis on the trade-off places economists in the position of hypercritical commentators.

Meanwhile, disagreements are not out of the question in

the field of cost–benefit analysis either. The one commentator sees different sacrifices than the other. The door is open to selective observation. An increase in government expenditure in times of depression invokes numerous negative effects – see below – that proceed above all from the higher taxes and the possible increase in the budgetary deficit. Higher taxes, now or later, may have a very different impact, depending on who tells the story. The same holds for the deficit. Some observers also see sacrifices because bottlenecks occur on the labour market, if not now then soon, once the depression is over. Other observers regard the latter as unimportant – as long as there are many jobless people there can hardly be any question of alternative costs. We are thus confronted by the question of utilizable overcapacity, which may be answered differently. Supply-siders will be more inclined to incorporate sacrifices here than Keynesians. All these issues belong on the agenda of econometrics – a worn-out formula, but imperative.

Cost–benefit analysis should be accepted among economists (a normative statement). Provided that – and now another worn-out formula follows – we are aware of its limitations. These are to be found above all in uncertainty about the shadow prices. The new scarcity of fresh air, clean water and unpoisoned land is unpriced. The economist who compiles a policy advice about the establishment of an industrial estate, the construction of a road, the extension of an airport, the reclamation of a polder, must incorporate prices of the natural environment that quantify the exchange. That is no easy task. The shadow prices carry a heavy normative load, and they are established in a colligative context. Never trust a cost–benefit analysis that presents itself as 'objective'. It is a useful method of enumerating things and localizing differences of opinion. It is a rationalistic technique, but the irrational element cannot be expelled. Economics cannot establish that the action groups demonstrating against the extension of Frankfurt Airport are wrong. As a citizen I should like to condemn these actions on account of their violent nature. As an economist, I hope that these undemocratic riots can be avoided by a sensible discussion. As an environmentalist I hope that the airport will not be extended and that air traffic will diminish. In that discussion economists can play a part by describing the alternatives as closely as possible and giving them price-tags. Let us hope that the feasible area within which the decision is taken becomes smaller. The citizens have the last word.

3.   A final complication in the separation between means and ends is to be found in the reasonings that establish the connection between the two. This connection may be a formalized decision model – that is of course the best – or a story, but there is always a colligative context. Even formal models are charged at those places where econometrics has not yet been able to indicate really hard relations. This is a sad state of affairs, because the separation between means and ends is precisely intended to demarcate a private area for science, where strictly falsifiable statements may be made, with on the other side of the fence the unfalsifiable exclamations of the citizens and the politicians. The fence does not prove to be a strict demarcation.

The latter imperfection assumes interesting forms when the decision model is in the hands of the policy-makers themselves (as in the United Kingdom and the Netherlands) and when it may be suspected that the model will be slightly distorted to produce desired results. The Keynesian models of the Fifties made insufficient allowance for the creation of liquidities and for what was happening on the capital market. By introducing these causal factors a more realistic picture was created, but simultaneously a certain resistance to policy. Via these newly introduced relations an increase in the budgetary deficit can have a restraining effect on investments. The result of this is that tax cuts intended to stimulate spending have a much smaller net effect than had been thought at first. A government that gives priority to reduction of the budgetary deficit can arm itself against criticism by influencing the model. This question pops up, of course, in the great political debate of the Eighties.

For if we now try to review the disagreements that occur on economic policy, we must again stress that every measure, large or small, is the issue of a conflict of interests. Every road that is built, every subsidy that is suggested, or done away with, every measure in the field of public health, has its natural proponents and opponents. Interests are always served and always harmed. That often gives the debate great ferocity. The arguments are always partly of an economic nature, and thus economists are always involved in the debate. That is excellent, if only from the point of view of professional employment, so long as one doesn't think that science is speaking. The pressure groups have their say, with the assistance of their economic advisers. They plead their case.

A spectacular form of the conflict of interests is the conflict of nations. We owe a number of interesting tenets to it: the doctrine of comparative costs, the infant industry argument, the theory of the optimum exchange rate, of the optimum currency area, of the optimum foreign exchange reserves (3). But the disputes continue to rage in politics. The old nationalism is constantly lying in wait in the form of protection, the pursuit of too large foreign exchange reserves, subsidization of national activities, dumping of toxic waste on the neighbours (in the Rhine!) and in the shared sea. Strangely enough, the open conflict flares up the most in the agencies that have been introduced precisely to foster harmony. The strongest example of this paradox is the European Community, which in essence serves a common purpose, viz the build-up of a growing European economy with free trade and free movement of persons. In fact the EEC is the scene of bitter strife. The conflict on national contributions to the common exchequer and the row about the common agricultural policy threaten to bring an end to the Community, without the economists being able to pronounce the spell that would save it. Perhaps it is as well to bear in mind the rather hopeless nature of these debates and to compare it with the debates between scientists – the latter are after all a good deal cooler and more businesslike, and they present the prospect of a possibly progressive science.

When, in the midst of all these coarse conflicts of interests, we consider the great political issues about which colligative economics might perhaps have something sensible to say, we arrive in my opinion at three of these. In increasing importance they are (a) the lively debate between the Keynesian expansionists and the restrictionists on employment; (b) the disagreement fought on various fronts between the supporters of the welfare state and their egalitarian friends on the one hand and the opponents of the welfare state and the elitists on the other; (c) the latent but very deeply rooted difference of opinion between the environmental activists and the observers who are of the opinion that damage to the environment is unpleasant but an acceptable price of progress. The debates under (b) and (c) are too complex to be properly discussed in this essay. I shall confine myself here to the problem under (a), related as it is to the two plausible stories told in Chapter IX (4). It should, however, be remarked that the three issues are interrelated. Anyone who has sombre views about the potential catastrophe threatening us via the environment is usually a firm supporter of the welfare state. Supporters of elitism often take a rather light-hearted view of pollution. There is also a connection with nationalism: the hypothesis that elitism and nationalism go hand in hand seems justified. These interweavings of the points of view indicate once again that colligation dominates thinking. People associate clusters of viewpoints into a whole that fits in with their experiences, their temperament and their beliefs. This gives birth to ideology: the political translation of a view of the world.

Ideologies are usually spoken of disapprovingly, and rightly so. They often consist of a mixture of prejudice, rigidity, cognitive dissonance and hollow rhetoric. They are often aimed at action and not at understanding. These two objectives may collide, and then insight is subordinated to the desire to change the world or, worse still, to maintain the existing political system by suppressing criticism. Marxism is an example of the two. In democratic countries Marxism criticizes free-enterprise production from a one-sided metaphor – the class struggle. In the countries where the Marxist dictatorship is established dissension is smothered in psychiatric hospitals. It is additionally repugnant that both forms of anti-science occur in the name of science.

This having been said, it must be admitted that the ideology can occasionally bear cognitive fruits. A Marxist colligator may be inspired to examine observable abuses. The paradigmatic hard core may yield a research programme that increases insight and acts as an eye-opener. Discrimination against ethnic groups and against women can be brought to light. Low wages among migrants can be exposed. The vicious circles of urban decay can be mapped. The Marxist ideologists often tackle problems that others leave untouched. For that reason journals such as the *Review of Radical Political Economics, Critique, The Cambridge Journal of Economics,* must be welcomed.

But of course, the ideology may very well be of a respectable nature, and contribute to the efficiency of spiritual life. It enables people to oversee policy problems quickly. Supercolligation may then fall outside the domain of science, but it saves energy. It enables people to overlook complex problems and reduce them to simple binary issues. It is part of their identity.

If the latter is true we have stumbled across the reason

why all adults are economists. A person must know who
he or she is, who his or her friends are, which nationality
he or she possesses, to which subgroups he or she belongs,
which common ideals bind him or her to other people.
Identity comprises someone's preferences in food – that is
why we are so often told that the speaker likes wine or exactly the opposite (I'm a teetotaller), which places he or she
has visited (I've never been to the Soviet Union or Greece
and I don't wish to go there either) and other irrelevancies.
*In economicis* we have numerous ideas, about our work,
our income, the chance of employment and dismissal, the
justification for that work, its future, and what governments must do and not do.That economic identity is a part
of ourselves. The professional economist differs from non-
economists in that somewhat more reasoning is at the bottom of these ideas, perhaps a little more knowledge of observables, somewhat more insight into unseen relations.
But these are smooth transitions.

Every economist practises his or her profession on the
basis of this supercolligation. A case could be made for ren-
dering it explicit before someone starts to unfold abstract
theories. To satisfy this requirement a small list follows of
my own prejudices. Personally I am an adherent to the
anti-nationalistic, egalitarian and pro-environment ideology. As a result, I have a quick opinion about the Olympic
Games (against), reclamation of nature areas (against), a
strict anti-pollution policy (for), a restrictive monetary policy aimed at breaking the power of the unions (against),
population growth (against), air traffic (against), Ronald
Reagan (against) social benefit for jobless and sick persons

who are not below the minimum wage (for), an incomes
policy (for), a generous policy for the arts (for), Israel (for),
the class struggle (against). As I said, not a single thinking
citizen escapes such super-colligative thought processes.
Only, it is advisable to keep a close watch on them.

(1)Mishan has made a brave attempt to defend his point of view that welfare economics has a normative tendency against P. Hennipman, who ad-
heres to the impossibility of the jump from *is* to *ought*. However, in doing
so Mishan has withdrawn to a position that is smaller than a pin's head:
value judgments on allocation are possible when there is a perfect consensus on them in a society. I'll bet. In that case the problem has disappeared.
But a world with a perfect political consensus – is that what we see around
us? E.J. Mishan, The Implications of Alternative Foundations for Welfare
Economics, and P. Hennipman, Mishan's Halfway House, *De Economist*,
132, No. 1, 1984, p. 75 ff.
(2)*On the Theory of Economic Policy,* Amsterdam, 1952.
(3)See H. Jager, *De behoefte aan internationale monetaire reserves als uit-
vloeisel van optimale economische politiek,* Groningen, 1981.
(4)It would be quite feasible to tell two plausible stories about (A) the
growth of real income since the Middle Ages, which reduces poverty, gives
people more play, serves culture and forms the basis for the welfare state.
This is the tale about the economic side of the march of civilization. Versus (B), the senseless forcing-up of production, which does not make people happier because wants are carried along by the preference drift
(B.M.S. van Praag) and the reference drift (A. Kapteyn), while in the interim nature is poisoned, nuclear energy descends upon us, people become
increasingly nervous, frustration leads to crime. Both tales can be supported by selective evidence. Story A is illustrated by figures on life expect-
ancy, the level of education, pictures of modern architecture, industrial
design, modern libraries, concert halls, the furnishings of middle-class
homes in the Western world, and all this compared with the situation in
1900. Story B – well, we know that: urban decay, poisoned land, drugs,
riots. Here too, just as in Chapter IX, a kind of synthesis could be attempted, which for instance can summon up the question: in which year,
in the U.S., the U.K., France and the Netherlands, did the turning point
appear at which the costs of the growth of GNP became higher than the

benefits? Was it 1960, or 1970, or 1980? Or will it be 1990, if we don't take care? I have been tempted to add such a chapter, but it would have been even more inconclusive than the rest.

Chapter XI

---

## BUDGETS: TOWARDS A NEW CONSENSUS?

Politics is coloured by strife, especially if interests and free-floating ideologies collide. It is therefore surprising that in most countries of Western Europe and in the United States a slight consensus is beginning to form about the broad outlines of economic recovery and how it has to be promoted. Most politicians agree that we must manage to attain higher growth rates. That is good for employment, for the Third World, and even for the environment (because a continued depression stands in the way of a sharp, selective reallocation policy, which in the short term costs jobs). Without selective growth no welfare state and no rehabilitation of the environment.

Most politicians also agree on a number of instruments. Better incentives, reflected in remuneration differentials between people of differing performance, have even received the consent of some egalitarians. There is a rather wide consensus about the desirability of increasing capital investments. Profit recovery may lay claim to the cautious approbation of at least some left-wing citizens. With regard to the policy instruments there is a difference of opinion, but in practice this is limited because in many cases the instruments cannot be applied. Thus many economists are in favour of an incomes policy or, more in particular, a planned wage policy, but they know very well that such a policy is frustrated by legal objections and by a lack of co-operation on the part of the unions. Some British commentators have also thought up the idea that a strict protectionist policy can save the United Kingdom, but that is inconsistent with GATT and the European Community, and would also lead to retaliation. Hard reality reduces the feasibility of imaginative possible policies. Most economists are realistic enough to see that.

The most curious field in which rapprochement occurs is budgetary policy. After all, neoclassicists and neo-Keynesians have a different story about this. The former want to reduce the government's role, the latter want to use the budget to activate the circulation. Despite attempts to arrive at a synthesis, that difference remains in essence, and it colours all debates about macro-issues. But even in budgetary policy it is true to say that topical developments and new insights have led to a convergence of practical policy proposals. This is inspired by two things: the inverted Haavelmo effect and the alarming effects of the strongly growing public debt.

The inverted Haavelmo effect concerns the influence of increased public expenditure that is fully covered by taxes. In the older neo-classical view this is nothing but a shift in allocation; higher public expenditure takes the place of private consumption or private investments. The effect on national income is zero. Haavelmo has demonstrated in a mini-model that national income can increase by the amount of the increase in expenditure to the extent that taxes are for the account of savings. This is hyper-Keynesian thinking. The Haavelmo effect is not without practical importance, but explains above all why, in times of over-spending, an expansion of the budgets leads to an increase in overspending. In times of tranquillity the increase in level of the public sector may perhaps stimulate growth a little, but that happens only because demand is aroused. No allowance is made for supply-side effects. In fact the Haavelmo effect acts as a provocation on supply-siders, and they have had no difficulty in inverting it.

The simplest way of doing so is to assume that investments will be adversely affected by higher taxation. This hypothesis even fits into a Keynesian reasoning, because in the latter investments depend on expectations concerning after-tax profits, and these in turn react to higher tax rates. If the regression coefficient of these reactions is high enough, the Haavelmo effect disappears; at a higher value it is inverted. In that case increases in the level of the budget lead to a contraction of national income. The latter result can be intensified by assuming that the greater burden of taxation reduces the incentive to work. And a very special reaction is incorporated by the hypothesis that higher taxes lead to higher wage claims which cannot be passed on in prices. In the latter case the Ricardian dictum that 'a tax on wages is a tax on profits' applies.

The question is how all these possibilities work out empirically. Research has been done into this by A. Knoester (1), who has tested a model with 31 equations for four countries (Germany, the Netherlands, the U.K. and the U.S.A.) for the period 1960–1980. Knoester finds balanced budget multipliers lying near to zero. That is to say, if no

additional wage claims are made to compensate for the increased tax on workers or consumers. If the latter is in fact
the case, the multipliers become negative. Thus a balanced
budgetary increase of 1% in the United States leads after
five years to a reduction of production of 1.8%. The result
for the U.K. is $-1.3\%$, for Germany $-2.1\%$ and for the
Netherlands no less than $-2.7\%$. Private employment falls
by figures between 1% and 1.9%. These results are more or
less in line with what supply-siders assert. They give no in-
dication that we are in the right-hand part of the Laffer
curve, but nevertheless they are not encouraging for those
who want to overcome the stagnation by increasing the size
of the public sector, and certainly not for those who levy
additional taxes for that purpose. The level of taxes and social contributions has risen in practically all countries; only
the U.K. is an exception. These percentages of GNP lie between 40% for the U.S.A. and 65% for the Netherlands.
They display a tendency towards uncontrolled growth.
That creates alarm. The wing of the Keynesians that deliberately wants to force up the level of the budget does not
have luck on its side.

But, it may be countered, the balanced-budget Keynesians follow an out-of-the-way reasoning – who wants to
raise taxes in a depression? It is much more consistent with
the Keynesian view to expand government expenditure
without tax increases. This policy advice too is at variance
with neo-classical views, and it could be expected that serious political disputes could arise between policy-oriented
economists on this, but that is hardly the case.

The reason for this is that the Keynesian proposals were

automatically implemented in the late Seventies and the Eighties. Everywhere public expenditure grew, everywhere taxes lagged behind it, everywhere budgetary deficits increased. Around 1980 these deficits still looked manageable: between 1% of GDP (France, U.S.A.) and 4% (the Netherlands, Japan), with Italy out of line (8%). But in the Eighties the depression struck. Expenditure rose, above all the transfer expenditure, the subsidies to firms, the interest on the national debt. Simultaneously, the proceeds of taxation were disappointing. Deficits doubled in four years' time. Deficits of some 10% of GNP were no longer an exception: in addition to Belgium and Italy, Sweden, the Netherlands, Denmark and Canada entered this zone. In France and the U.S.A. too increases in the direction of 4–5% of GNP occurred. (Exception: the U.K.: the balance fell to 2.5%).

Now it is part of the Gestalt of orthodox Keynesians not to worry about these deficits. They can be financed out of the surplus savings of the private sector, of which they form the mirror-image. They do not constitute a burden for the future. They pay for themselves because they drive up national income. But in the Eighties this lightheartedness began to falter badly. The neo-classicists, who had always distrusted public borrowing, had right on their side. The Keynesians too were afraid of the high indebtedness. Thus a new kind of consensus came about: they met each other halfway. That came about through three things: the rising interest rate, the growing debt : income ratio and the most alarming events in the sphere of international high finance.

The strongly rising interest rate in the Seventies is a controversial phenomenon as regards the explanation for it, but everyone agrees that it is to be deplored. An interest rate of 15% in the U.S.A., 10% in Germany and the Netherlands and 12% in the U.K. (the situation at the beginning of the Eighties) is not good. Such rates aggravate stagnation. Whether the high rate is a reflection of inflation and of inflationary expectations, or a result of a tight money policy, or a consequence of the possession that governments take of the capital market – that can be debated, but it is better to take no risks and to pursue a reduction of interest. There is a striking consensus about this. In that policy there is no place at all for deliberate increases in the budgetary deficit.

A second reason for growing consensus is that budgetary deficits have the unpleasant property of increasing the public debt. Moreover, that has a cumulative effect, because on a larger debt higher interest has to be paid. The subject lends itself both to alarming applications of logic and to colligation. As regards logic, one can think above all of the simple formula which states that the ratio between the total public debt $D$ and national income $Y$ grows towards a value $z/y$, in which $z$ is the deficit as a fraction of national income and $y$ the growth rate of national income (2). If $z = 5\%$ and $y = 5\%$, and those are not unreal figures in conditions of stagnation-with-a-bit-of-inflation, we are heading for a national debt that is as large as national income. At an interest rate of 10%, 10% of $Y$ is then transferred from the taxpayer to the government's creditors – a transfer that comes on top of all other transfers of which the welfare state has such a wide variety.

A value of $D/Y = 100\%$ is not yet a frequent occurrence
in the Western world, but some countries have displayed
increases that cause anxious observers to fear the worst.
Belgium is the worst off; there the debt : income ratio in
1974 was still a fairly comfortable 50%, but an uncontrolled financial policy has driven the ratio up to nearly
100%, and the end of the increase is not yet in sight. In the
Netherlands $D/Y$ has risen in ten years' time from 40% to
60%, and the rise is continuing. Over that period Germany
displays an increase from 20 to 35%. The U.K. is a case
apart – there $D/Y$ fell, from a high level in 1974, namely
67%, to about 50% now, but that was accompanied by a
highly stagnating production and a sharply increasing unemployment. (In the U.K. the debate among economists on
optimum policy is the most violent.) A more cheerful case
is that of Switzerland, where $D/Y$ remained practically constant at the low level of 30%. Everyone looks enviously at
this example, and tries to learn from it.

The United States forms a very special and interesting
case. There the debt : income ratio remained fairly stable
at 50% in the Seventies. In the Eighties three things happened simultaneously. A sweeping tax reduction was carried through in 1981, the rates of personal taxation being
reduced by 23%. That ties in with the preferences of the
Reagan Administration. Meanwhile the depression struck,
as a result of which the tax base shrank. However, the
planned reduction in expenditure did not come about – on
the contrary. The increases in the military budgets were not
compensated for by reductions elsewhere, though attempts
were made to do so. These three factors together drove up

the budgetary deficit. In 1980 it was still 50 billion dollars; in 1984 it was nearly 200 billion, or almost 6% of national income. At a growth rate of national income that is barely higher than 6% this is quickly pushing the $D/Y$ ratio into the Belgian situation. This rapid increase in the deficit is sharply criticized by commentators who can be seen as supporters of Reagan. In particular Martin Feldstein, the chairman of the Council of Economic Advisers, has displayed serious concern about the budgets in 1984. He expects that the deficit can still double. This news was presented to the American public under the title *America's Black Hole* (*Time,* March 5, 1984, with an extremely evocative cover, showing dollars disappearing into a yawning abyss).

Feldstein resigned in May 1984 and saddled the Reagan Administration with some embarrassment. It could hardly be pleased by the suggestion that it acquiesces in big holes and black abysses. Nor does it like the idea that it pushes up the interest rate. For the latter the Fed is blamed. Concerning the black hole the Administration took the unusual step – unusual in a conservative colligative context – of showing that the budgetary deficit does not matter much or even that it does not exist. You have only to take a somewhat closer and more sophisticated look at it and it disappears. Subtract the cyclical component; look at the entire public sector and not just at the Federal Government; and correct the Government interest payments for inflation. You will find that the U.S. Government actually runs a structural surplus. This imaginative piece of reasoning was presented on May 23, 1984, to the surprised readers of the *Backgrounder,* an official USIS publication (3). The Keynesian heritage, though not explicitly mentioned in this document, seems to exert some influence in U.S. Government circles. Still, the argument will not convince everybody. Too few people read the *Backgrounder*, a useful though somewhat lopsided source of information.

While this whole discussion is in itself hardly conducive to lightheartedness regarding debt policy, yet a third reason joins the list: the international situation. National governments borrow on a capital market which is open on all sides. Their bonds are in the hands of people of all kinds of nationalities and of transnational bodies. Small shifts in the portfolios may have serious consequences for the prices of the bonds. If the investors turn against a country – particularly a small country – it can no longer have recourse to the international market, or only at a much higher interest rate. Refinancing of redeemed loans then becomes difficult or impossible. This bogey hangs like a dark cloud over a government's financial policy. A loss of confidence can start an avalanche. This intimidating possibility must moreover be seen against the background of the gigantic debts that Latin American countries have incurred – borrowing there has run wild, there is no question of repayment, and interest obligations cannot be met. The example is not worthy of emulation. A collapse of the international credit system haunts the dreams of financiers.

Black holes, dark clouds, avalanches, collapse. Those are the metaphors by which public finance is described in the Eighties (4). They have a wide scope, are barely falsifiable and create a psychological atmosphere in which Keynesian proposals for the deliberate increasing of expenditure without adequate financial cover have no chance. There is not a single politician of a government party – with the opposition it is different – who finds such proposals attractive. Economists cannot recommend them, because they cannot properly foresee the effects of a growing national debt. Even the desire for tax cuts, which is strongly felt both by supply-siders – they want to reduce the *wedge* between what a person earns and what a person gets – and by Keynesians, and which is supported by populistic Reaganomists, is not well received by most commentators. What in fact happens is that governments, in their fear of increasing the public debt, increase the burden of taxation, although that in no way fits in with their own intentions, nor with the promises that they tend to make to the electorate. Everywhere the feeling exists that the policy scope for budgetary policy is minimum, and that this extremely limited scope is consumed by the automatic forces summoned up by the stagnation itself.

What is the conclusion from this brief consideration of budgetary policy in the Eighties? Chiefly this: whereas many critics of the economists' stance on policy assume that all political decisions are the subject of dispute, notably decisions involving colliding economic interests (agricultural policy, protection, construction of nuclear power plants), we see here a case in which a certain degree of consensus comes into being – and that between two large ideological schools of thought that are theoretically opposed to one another. That seems a paradox. It is, however, an illustration of the way in which economic reality can drive parties into each other's arms. While the ideologists debate, the practical economists find one another in their capacity of worried citizens. There is consolation here for the profession, insofar as it believes that a mainstream exists, not only in economic theory but also in the *praxis* of macropolicy.

(1)A. Knoester, Stagnation and the Inverted Haavelmo Effect: Some International Evidence, *De Economist,* 131, No. 4, 1983, p. 548.

(2)E.D. Domar, The Burden of the Debt and the National Income, *American Economic Review,* December, 1947, p. 798.

(3)United States Information Service, May 23, 1984. The report was prepared by M.J. Bailey, G. Balabanis, G. Tavlas and M. Ulan under the direction of A. Allen Wallis, Undersecretary of State for Economic Affairs. The report also tells us that budget deficits perhaps do raise interest rates a bit, though this effect is very uncertain, but if they do 'they do it while at the same time stimulating spending and so contributing to economic recovery'. A Keynesian fifth column in the Reagan Administration? Or proof that economists really are a cool, well-integrated crowd who know how to build bridges between seemingly opposing viewpoints? Or just another example that one can have an opinion from the profession provided that one is willing to pay for it?

(4)Lightheartedness about these matters is additionally discouraged in countries with a Germanic language because the same word is used for debt and guilt. The conscience is involved, and original sin. In the opening chorus of the St. Matthew Passion the choir sing: 'Sehet! Wohin? Auf unsere Schuld'. This is what Feldstein could say to Reagan if the gentlemen spoke to each other in German, which is probably not the case.

Chapter XII

# METHODOLOGICAL STATEMENTS

Economists have long debated methodological questions (1). We owe to that such stimulating books as Benjamin Ward's *What's Wrong with Economics* (New York, London, 1972) and Mark Blaug's *The Methodology of Economics or How Economists Explain* (Cambridge, 1980). I mention these two books because they are conceived in an opposite spirit, and because I find both of them appealing. They present a starting point for broaching an important methodological moot point, the only one that I want to discuss here (2).

Ward, the man who transferred the concept of colligation from the science of history to economics, points to the 'richness of our experience' which is 'captured most fully and accurately in the hands of a great storyteller' (p. 244). He upbraids neo-classical and Marxist economics for having a weak and implausible picture of mankind; he wants research into the actual patterns of human behaviour. He considers that economics has wrongly distanced itself from the subjects studied, whom he calls 'economees', and that logical positivism is to blame for this (3). Ward also welcomes the richness of language, and is of the opinion that the technical language of the mainstream economists leads to an impoverishment in communication and observation.

*Jan Pen*

Blaug, on the other hand, supports Popper. He makes short shrift of storytelling: 'it lacks rigor, lacks a definite logical structure, it is all too easy to verify and virtually impossible to falsify. It is or can be persuasive because it never runs the risk of being wrong' (p. 127). Blaug advocates work 'addressed to the same set of questions that preoccupy the neo-classical scientific research program' (p. 264). He wants 'discrimination between wheat and chaff'. His emphasis falls on falsification. And finally Blaug is concerned with prediction: 'Orthodox economics can indeed boast that it has increased the economist's capacity for making predictions. At the same time, it must be emphasized how limited this capacity is even now' (p. 262). According to Blaug – and here Ward would agree – economists still tend too much towards 'analytical elegance, economy of theoretical means, and the widest possible scope obtained by ever more heroic simplification'. Priority must be given to 'predictability and significance for policy questions' (p. 259).

It is striking that both Ward and Blaug make normative statements on the question of how economists ought to think. Moreover, they make statements on how economists ought not to think. It is the latter, negative part of their conclusions that gives the debate a certain sharpness. The hook can easily be removed by observing a little more tolerance. It might very well be that economists follow the recommendations of both Blaug and Ward, in the sense that some concentrate more on the narrative method and others on empirical research. This seems a cheap way to settle disputes, but there is no better one. There is no good reason why both subcultures could not co-exist. And there are good reasons why they need one another.

For every good story implies falsifiable statements. A story without structure belongs in the pub, and even there it is not appreciated. Every decent story refers to observable facts, a selection is made, logic is practised, parameters are implied. That is all falsifiable or at least disputable. Also woven into it are value judgments, which are not falsifiable, though they can be made explicit in a discussion. In that case the discussion must of course take place; the parties must not turn their backs on each other in disgust. That is the great danger which the purists summon up: their scientific rigour leads to elimination of the debate with the public, and to a *rigor mortis* in communication. Economists must deliberately learn to handle debate. They should be trained to recognize value judgments for what they are. In a story metaphors are used, and there we encounter one of the most troublesome elements in the debate: high impact, low falsifiability, and investigated much too little by the economic profession, which often pulls a face as if it had never heard of a metaphor.

The narrative, humanistic practice of economics may never look down on empirical research – the latter must supply the parameters that give the story its backbone. It is the quantitative researchers, and more particularly the econometricians, who do the hard work. They test the models and supply the numerical values that form the core of every economic tale worth listening to. And these researchers shift the dividing line from what we only suspect towards what we really know. There is a good deal that we cannot predict at all – an example: what the influence will be of increases in the budgetary deficit on future national income – but quantitative research perhaps shifts the dividing line between unpredictable and predictable to some extent. Lord Kelvin's endeavour to quantify everything that is relevant may have been too ambitious if applied to economics, but it must be held in esteem, also by colligators.

Conversely, the mathematical economists and the econometricians must not look down on the colligators. I admit that the temptation to do so is considerable – many stories consist of a mixture of ignorance and lukewarm air, they border on demagogy and they are told with dubious intentions. The intention is often only to write a best-seller, and that sometimes succeeds too (4). But without narrative economics the hard work of the real researchers has little point. Who is interested in the reliability of a regression equation if nothing can be done with it in a coherent story? Who cares if parameters are found of equations that are of little relevance? Who is the slightest bit interested in simple figures such as national income, the price level, the Herfindahl–Hirschman Concentration Index, if they do not lead to a kind of view of things? It would be much better if the econometricians were to concern themselves for once with the art of storytelling, in order to separate wise and foolish stories from each other. This does occur – an example is William Nordhaus' attack on the computer runs of Jay Forrester and Dennis Meadows in their *Limits to growth* (5) – but it ought to occur more often. A dialogue between the two subcultures is desired. The econometricians must criticize and improve stories, and the narrative school must ask questions of the econometricians – supply me if you can with the parameters that indicate the influence of the fear that politicians have of the national debt.

Such a discussion between subcultures is not only intended to further peace. One of the intentions is that the number of explanations and stories decreases. Their number is too great. This leads to indetermination – stories standing side by side – and to overdetermination – stories that are at variance with one another. A good example is formed by the stagnation of the Seventies, which can be explained by incidental shocks, overinvestment, underconsumption, overtaxation, wage inflation, price inflation, technical slowdown, rigidity of institutions, softening of people, lack of confidence. We can tell stories about a natural reaction to excessively high growth; a process of recovery; the beginning of the end (6). All plausible, not all equally convincing, and in part contradictory. Every view contains prejudice, but also verifiable hypotheses. We have too many of them. The problem is not that economists cannot explain the facts; on the contrary, too many theories are chasing the same facts. This overdetermination can disappear only by falsification, a cruel but hygienic activity. This intolerance is necessary, for we are dragging too dead a weight of old views around with us. They are restraining the progress of thought and they have to be rejected. However, that doesn't help much, as long as we cannot convince the adherents to those superseded views that they are wrong.

The latter point brings us to one of the least recognized methodological problems: that of rhetoric. The word is associated with a civilized but superficial pastime, or with insincere striving after effect. Rhetoric is often regarded as a debate for debate's sake, fancy speechifying, affected figures of speech, many metaphors of course, graceful gestures; not to be taken seriously. This negative view leads us away from the Aristotelian interpretation, in which rhetoric is a method for finding the truth (7). An attempt to increase the respectability of rhetoric among economists has recently been undertaken by Donald M. McCloskey. In *The Rhetoric of Economics* (8) he advocates in the first place recognition of the fact that economists use rhetoric even if they say they don't, and in the second place recognition of its advantages. As such McCloskey mentions better writing, better teaching, better public relations, better econometrics (the latter invoking C. Sims). 'Be not afraid!', he cries out to us (p. 508). A revaluation of rhetoric need not lead to the abandonment of science, and he turns against Mark Blaug and Imre Lakatos, who in his opinion have a spasmodic dislike of what they regard as irrationalism. According to McCloskey rhetoric is not irrational and we must have confidence in the trend of the discussion.

However, the latter is begging the question. McCloskey herewith voices the hope that science makes progress in the course of the debate, but that hope is justified only if the participants follow strict rules – and those he does not discuss. Worse still, he champions Paul Feyerabend, whose *Against Method: Outline of an Anarchistic Theory of Knowledge* (London, 1975) is a stimulating book, but stimulating in a dubious direction. Feyerabend gives an interesting description of the creative process, in which things happen much less strictly than some severe methodologists would have us believe – chaos and poetry and unknown impulses dominate creativity, and there is nothing against that. But Feyerabend creates the impression that the results of all that creativity ought not to be subject to rules. That seems to me to be a misconception. We may be extremely tolerant where the *ars inveniendi* is concerned – but we must be as strict as possible with the *ars iudicandi*. If we abandon the latter requirement, and apply 'anything goes' to assertions, we open the door to the wildest nonsense and to ideologists and demagogues. Feyerabend creates the impression that he enjoys this nonsense. Well, McCloskey should not have spoken sympathetically about it. In this way he undermines his own argument.

For rhetoric's task, to use Blaug's expression, is to separate the wheat from the chaff. Even as sceptics, we must keep on seeking indisputable truths. In doing so it is useful for us to realize that these are to be found in some of our seven compartments – at least nearly! – in others less so and in others again not at all. That is the purport of this essay. But the debate between economists (and between economists and citizens) takes place in all compartments, whether we like it or not.

That confronts us with the methodological dilemma: do we, as economists, want to participate or not? It is quite feasible for an economist to say: 'I am falling back on logic (where I am always right) or on empiricism (where I encounter only the econometricians as partners in a dialogue), and I am leaving everything that is soft and weak to the citizens, the politicians, the journalists. To John Kenneth Galbraith ('he knows a lot of economics for a layman'), Milton Friedman ('travelling salesman in political software'), Lester Thurow ('less thorough'), George Gilder ('sic'). They are at best rhetoricians, and I, I'm a scientist, in the spirit of Popper'. It is a tenable position. Except that Popper wrote a book under the title: *The Open Society and its Enemies* (London, 1945) – a rather colligative case against the Marxists and the Hegelians. Popper's argument played a convincing role in a political discussion. For that is the point: the discussion continues nevertheless, without the participants having sought the methodologists' permission. The participants follow their own rhetoric and the debate is conducted in the street.

It is a great temptation to choose the safe solution: economists withdraw to the castle of logic, and leave even empiricism to others. This is the view that has been best formulated by T.W. Hutchison: economics as a box of tools (9). But others too feel the temptation: Alfred Marshall spoke of a 'machine for the discovery of truth'; he did something with that machine, and wasn't that science? John Neville Keynes used the words: 'a method rather than a doctrine'. This purism leads, as an extreme consequence, to books with definitions, classifications, algebra and graphs; not to genuine theories, for they have already been tainted by reality.

The other possibility is that the economists take part in a debate which they know to be full of unscientific elements. If they find this disgusting, they can make for themselves the mental reservation that they are present in their capacity of citizens (and they should not conceal that reservation, even if it damages their prestige). Participation has the advantage that certain rules can be imposed on rhetoric. And they should not then be the rules that aim at maximum effect, but at the search for truth. Good rhetoric is the rhetoric of the *vir bonus* (10). An economist breaks the rules of rhetoric if he or she selects his or her facts in an immoral way and overlooks the position of the poor (11). Or if he or she is heedless of the decline of the environment, with the argument 'we cannot measure it'. The rules are broken when misleading metaphors are used: 'society is a prison' (Foucault). Or when tautological statements are explained normatively: 'people are rational' (Stigler). Such rhetorical artifices are contrary to moral standards. Anyone who believes that our present society is a battleground is a bad person or a desperate person, or both.

There the nightmare of the positivists thus looms up before us in all its hideousness: *economics as a Moral Science*. That is exactly what we were trying to get rid of! Detached from the church, detached from politics, detached from the moralists and the ideologists with their unacceptable prescriptions! We are being shoved back in that direction by the adherents to colligation and rhetoric – a relapse to dark times. This fright seems understandable to me. We need not accept the conclusion that the economic debate is a moral debate. We can make a choice against colligation and rhetoric. But then that has its price, namely that economists talk among themselves and with non-economists only about the things that they know for certain. The only commitment then relates to science, and that is a cool affair in the present state of the art.

For those who, other than I, choose the latter solution,

a word of consolation. Economics possesses a huge arsenal of near-certainties. They have been constantly under consideration in the above. They fall into the category of observations and logic, and to a smaller extent into the empirical category, although there the signs of the regression coefficients are at least usually clear. Economists can even have a careful say about policy, with little self-assurance, but the contribution is a useful one. There is a tremendous amount still to be done. Perhaps there will be exciting things to discover; the logical proposition, supported by evidence, that under steady growth the increase in productivity is equal to technical progress divided by labour's share was after all *also* exciting. We are in no way sitting with empty hands if we withdraw to the areas where our consensus and our certainties lie, and if we try to shift the frontiers. But it is not warm there.

(1)Anyone wishing to read a fine survey: J.J. Klant, *Rules of the Game, The Logical Structure of Economic Theories*, Cambridge, 1984.
(2)There are of course many more methodological disagreements than the one between the proponents and opponents of colligation. But in my opinion they are of less importance. One of them: must we try to integrate economics with political science, sociology, psychology; or must we keep a sharp watch on the borders? Anyone opting for colligation opts also for the former, and vice versa. This kind of methodological value judgment comes in clusters. It will not surprise the reader that I am not an advocate of a meticulous demarcation of economics; there are a lot of interesting things to do on the borderline. In fields like public finance this shows very clearly.
(3)Ward's reproach is partly unfounded. Some econometricians examine the behaviour and the consequences of the 'economees': anyone formulating and testing an investment equation is concerned with behaviour. B.M.S. van Praag is investigating psychical welfare, in direct contact with the human beings themselves.

(4)Take J.K. Galbraith, *The New Industrial State,* Boston, 1967. This story is unsound because it divides industry into two parts: the strong corporations that are not troubled by competition and are interwoven with governments, and the small businesses that operate in the market. The strong businesses are independent of the market; they plan their activities, control sales and are masters of their environment. Galbraith is of the opinion that traditional economic theory does not relate to the latter category. The bipartition is evocative and can be verified with examples – until one realizes that the giants of the automobile industry are quite definitely exposed to sharp market influences (e.g. Japanese competition), that they can contract against their will, totter on the brink of a precipice. This also applies to other giants, above all if they make capital goods. They can plan all they like, but they do not control the market, not even if they have the government as a customer – the latter is inclined to cut down on its purchasing during a recession. Firms with a strong market position doubtless exist, but they are not necessarily large and their position is concerned more with technical innovation than with control of sales. Now Galbraith's misleading story is fairly innocuous; but we hear of similar narratives about large enterprises that are malicious and impute all the world's evils to these concerns. Something of an exaggeration.

(5)William Nordhaus, World Dynamics: Measurement Without Data, *Economic Journal,* 1973, 332, p. 1156.

(6)See the special number of *De Economist* on Economic Stagnation, 1983, No. 4, which also includes the article by A. Knoester discussed above. In that number the most varied of views are expressed. They are partly complementary, and partly contradictory – which of the two is not always clear. That's a pity, for when contradiction occurs, at least one of the parties is wrong. Or so Descartes says.

(7)Aristotle ascribes disagreements to the difference in place (locus) from which the discussers regard a thing. Rhetoric aims at bringing this to light, and at creating a *locus communis.* This approach brings the truth to light: in the final stage of the discussion everyone observes the same thing. In the Roman tradition the goal changed. Rhetoric was practised by an orator, who had to try to induce the judge to pass a favourable verdict. Though not being a lawyer himself, the orator used legal arguments, but always with an eye to the effect that they had on the judge. Rhetoric becomes a practical and sometimes cynical affair, which has little to do with seeking truth and in which striving for effect and tricks are not disdained. The present emotional value of the term has been coloured by this picture: speeches of a dubious nature, but sometimes nevertheless very fine ones.

It is then incidentally forgotten that the ideal orator as decribed by Cicero
must not only seem to be a respectable man but must also *be* one *( vir bonus)*.

(8)D.M. McCloskey, The Rhetoric of Economics, *Journal of Economic
Literature,* 1983, No. 2, p. 481. The economists I know react rather nega-
tively to this article.

(9)T.W. Hutchison, *The Significance and Basic Postulates of Economic
Theory,* New York, 1938. In my opinion a box of tools may not be called
a theory.

(10)This *vir bonus* may be described in various ways. Ward says of his
'great storyteller': 'A human who has observed his fellows with sympathy
and self-recognition'. I should like to add to that: 'an economist who uses
the result of economic science in a decent manner'.

(11)A small example. Herbert Stein, chairman of Nixon's Council of Economic Advisers, says in A Calm View of the Economic Horizon (*Economic Impact,* No. 44, 1983/84) that the American economy in the Eighties,
though it has problems, is in good shape. 'The American economy is
healthy'; and 'probably only about 10% of the 10% who are unemployed
are in poverty' (p. 8). This statement relates not to facts but to stylized
facts; the stylization seems to me callous and morally reprehensible. This
is the wrong kind of rhetoric. Just as disgusting as the mathematics of a
certain Constantine Azariadis, who 'proves' that all unemployment is voluntary.

Chapter XIII

## MAINSTREAM, MUD PUDDLES

Suppose you're an economist and you're troubled by the questions that were repeatedly under discussion in earlier chapters: what can we say for certain? Are economists querulous? Does economics really exist, in the sense of a coherent whole of techniques and opinions, or is it one big confusion? Are we making progress towards an increasing consensus, or is the range of differing views steadily growing? Is our profession an honest one, or does our output consist of hokum? Answering such questions is a colligative undertaking, full of selective observation, freely moving logic, value judgments (for do we compare ourselves to physicists or to theologians?) and storytelling. And don't forget: the answers are influenced by what we like to hear (1).

A cheerful story about the broad-flowing mainstream is quite feasible. We must then first of all concentrate attention on the impressive analytical machinery and on economic mathematics. The mainstream comprises marginalistic micro-economics, which analyses the decisions of the individual actor: the inheritance of the *Grenznuetzler,* a widespread system of optimum conditions, under uncertainty and costly information (2). Next comes meso-economics, i.e. supply and demand on the market of more or less homogeneous goods; that is the inheritance of Marshall, enriched by the theory of imperfect competition, oligopoly, dynamic instability à la Hanau, speculation, market power. Then macro-economics à la Walras, which is micro-economics multiplied by *n,* and genuine macro-economics à la Wicksell–Keynes–Hicks–Hansen, with the possibility of underspending and overspending, and the matching stock adjustments à la Blinder and Solow. And of course macro-economics When Markets Do Not Clear (3). Finally mondo-economics, with the explanation of the international division of labour, the exchange rates, the balance of payments and the extreme differences in productivity between countries. This whole of micro-, meso-, macro- and mondo-economics is synthetic and eclectic. (Grumblers say that the parts fit badly together, but nothing's perfect.)

With this set of logical instruments in mind reality must be assessed, and in that diagnosis differences of opinion rear their head. They are of a colligative nature. The question of stability versus instability in particular divides minds. There are two possible stories, as outlined in Chapter IX. Sensible people can perhaps agree on a compromise: the economic world sometimes seems pleasantly stable, and at other moments does not. Sometimes one may have the very brief illusion that Walrasian equilibrium gives an approximate description of some peaceful corner of the real world, but usually it definitely does not. Usually disturbances are going on, which are compensated for or not. Compensation or cumulation, that is the question. What happens depends on the intensity of the shocks, on the structure – the value of the elasticities! – and on the policy followed. In reality shocks of a very different nature are always occurring: on the cost side, on the demand side, from technology, from changes in tastes, from psychological waves. It would be nice if things were different, but that's life. Political intervention – for instance legal intervention, new regulations – also has the unpleasant habit of overburdening reality. By selective observation everyone can build up his or her favourite view of history: a trend with aberrations, or a series of jolts, shocks, jumps and events. There is some truth in both stories. But it is not always easy to interpret the present situation in the light of history. As a result the mainstream suffers from a certain overdetermination. Too many theories exist side by side.

But, so says the optimistic story, overdetermination is not so bad. After all, there are many *repertoires* and we may hope that econometrics acts as a referee between rival hypotheses. That doesn't always work, but there is progress.

Further, the optimistic interpretation must definitely and emphatically refer to the empirical work that ranks somewhat lower than top-level econometrics, but is highly respectable: the stacks of books and reports by experts, produced daily, on specific situations: countries, branches of industry, regions, studies on special topics. They are published by a tremendous number of institutions, national and international. In other words, these are the publications of the central banks, the statistical offices, the government agencies, the EEC, the OECD, the UN. We must point to the work of the economists in their daily business of life, i.e. to agricultural economics, transport economics, town planning, cultural economics, environmental economics. We must above all keep a watch on the work of economists in firms. And on the many variants of cost–benefit analysis for public projects.

All this work is fairly uncontroversial. On the contrary, economic technology lessens the scope for decisions by furnishing information and by pointing to the positive and negative consequences of decisions. Economists who have never heard of Ken Cole, John Cameron and Chris Edwards (4), and are not aware of the metaphysical necessity for disagreement, ensure that hidden consequences of policy are brought to light, that substitutions and long-term effects that perhaps would have otherwise remained unnoticed are taken into account. Political debates are supplied with a foundation of factual information, system is introduced into the discussion, the debate is penetrated by a rationalistic spirit. Even ideological controversies about the best policy can be contained, with an occasional helping hand from hard practicability. This may be illustrated by the new consensus about budgetary policy. An uneasy and very imperfect consensus, but one just the same. Economics is a part of the knowledge industry, and not the worst part either.

If you reason like that, and conclude that there is much to be proud of, you need not deny that controversies exist, but there are methods of relativizing them. Firstly, by pointing to the political nature of these disputes. Citizens are speaking who are disguised as economists; advocates using economic arguments. In this disguise they tell one-sided tales, but that is no science. Secondly, attention may be drawn to alternative schools of thought. Those are the interesting accompaniments of 'normal science', and they have to be there to keep the debate going. Marxists and Maoists, extreme Austrians who try to explain everything by the rational individual, followers of Posner from the Law and Economics club, disciples of Ayn Rand, and the handful of contemporaries who want to abolish money and pursue full unemployment. This is the colourful fringe, partly lunatic but nevertheless interesting and useful for giving the mainstream perspective and us a good laugh. Normal science can occasionally pick up something useful from these fringe phenomena – the selection is made by the invisible college of scientists.

This optimistic story is defensible, but it can be inverted. The mainstream is in actual fact a Mud Puddle. If you want to prove this point, the following procedure is effective. Invite a number of protagonists from rival schools of thought; let each of them write a polemic; don't devote too much attention to the common elements in normal science; write an introduction and a coda in which the disagreements are emphasized again and add a few more moot points; and then entitle the collection *The Crisis in Economic Theory* (New York, 1982). This is the procedure followed by Daniel Bell and Irving Kristol, and the result is what was to be expected. (The image of the mainstream as a mud puddle has been taken from one of the authors of this collection, viz Edward J. Nell, who defends a sort of Marxist point of view. It is the type of metaphor that brings science into discredit. Nell's rhetoric is of the slightly poisonous kind.)

*Jan Pen*

One of the sad aspects of this collection of essays is the concentrated attack, from various sides, on Keynesian theory. That is in the fashion of the Seventies and Eighties, but it is not a good thing. Keynesian theory has shown how incomes and expenditure can throw each other out of gear, how underspending and overspending can be generated without anyone being to blame – consumers spend an income that varies and producers react to this by adapting their investments to the changing sales. The consequence is that total spending is now too great for the productive capacity and then too small again. It is not necessary to assume a stable multiplier. In fact, Keynesian theory shows how the multiplier can change systematically if the tax rate, the propensity to consume and the propensity to import change. Nor is it necessary to make special assumptions concerning a Phillips curve, the behaviour of the interest rate or that of prices and wages. The Keynesian interaction disturbs the homeostasis of a neo-classical world, and that is in agreement with many facts of life. Although – I have shown in the above that neo-classical cybernetics also does its work, and that the mix between the two is precisely one of the big problems of the present day. We do not get a grasp of that mix by banishing from our minds the destabilizing interaction of incomes and expenditure, and therefore anti-Keynesianism is a dogmatic, unproductive and regressive school of thought.

In *The Crisis of Economic Theory* this eclectic point of view is not advanced, or it is advanced too weakly, or in too complicated a form. Take the contribution by Frank Hahn, one of the best-known supporters of the disequilibrium school, and definitely someone who believes that neo-classical cybernetics has only limited force. He defends the Arrow–Debreu analysis of general equilibrium as a purely logical exercise, by pointing out that it is concerned with a proof of existence; this proof does not, of course, say that the world is also one of Walrasian equilibrium. On top of that, Hahn clearly states that prices alone can never determine the production plans of General Motors, 'simply because they know that they cannot sell (and buy) all they want at these prices' (p. 136). Hahn adds that non-perfect competition must be invoked to account for this. Certainly, but I should like to add: plus something Keynesian about national income. If we provide the automobile concern with the prices for a future year (including those of the Japanese competition!) plus the macro data, the managers can quite definitely compile a production plan. The reason why the Eighties have such a gloomy appearance in most countries is to be found in the volume of world trade, which is directly dependent on national incomes. Hahn would not have needed to emphasize this point if everyone knew it, but the latter is unfortunately not the case.

Next take the criticism by Allen H. Metzler in this collection. He is a monetarist and thus opposed to Keynes. But what are in fact his complaints? They prove to be about: (a) the alleged trade-off between inflation and unemployment; (b) guideposts and guidelines as instruments against inflation; and (c) the 'illusive output gap'. The first two of these are not directed against income–expenditure analysis; they are adventitious and moreover (b) is of a political nature; incidentally, those guideposts are rejected by many

Keynesians. Only (c) is relevant, for if there was no 'output gap' around 1980, there was no deficiency of demand either and we could put the Keynesian view under wraps. But is it now really true that the steel industry, shipbuilding, the automobile industry, are safeguarded against deficiency of demand? Are they suffering only from structural shifts, foreign competition, sluggish technology and overinvestment in the past? A likely story!

A stronger example of needless acerbity, but now directed against the neo-classicists. Israel Kirzner states, in the name of Neo-Austria, that the mainstream is 'seriously deficient in any genuine understanding of the working of market capitalism' (p. 111). He speaks of 'excessive preoccupation with equilibrium, an unfortunate perspective on competition, grossly insufficient attention to the role of knowledge, expectations and learning'. 'The entire theoretical structure needs reconstruction.' These are thus not the words of a Marxist or a Post Keynesian, but of a proponent of individualism. It is difficult to understand this vehement criticism in the light of all those studies on branches of industry (industrial economics), and I also recall many books on disequilibrium (Edmond Malinvaud!), imperfect competition, the role of knowledge, expectations and learning. Or does Kirzner place the still instructive book by Friedrich von Wieser, *Theorie der Gesellschaftlichen Wirtschaft* (1914) and all that follows from it (the work by the incredibly productive Fritz Machlup!) outside the mainstream? In other words, is there no 60% overlap between the Austrian School and the mainstream? Has Kirzner perhaps only the mathematics of Arrow and Debreu in mind?

In that case, we have here a rather limited view of all the things that economists do.

The most fundamental but least convincing criticism of the Keynesian view comes from the rational expectations (Ratex) school. Mark H. Willis presents their world of thought in an aggressive way; aggressive by demonstrating that Ratex means the end of everything that derives from Keynes. His essay provokes counter-aggression, and perhaps I may explain here what I have against this school of thought. It all seemed fairly innocuous as yet when John F. Muth introduced in 1961 the assumption that individuals make the best possible use of the information that is available on their environment (5). But it was not innocuous. For something rather special was assumed concerning the mental processes of people: they expect that prices will behave as predicted by the neo-classical theory, with a complete set of supply and demand equations. Excess supply and excess demand will influence prices, and that will soon make these disequilibria disappear. Muth's intention was therefore to show that the cobweb theorem is unsound; and that is definitely not an innocuous intention, for this theorem forms the basis of the dynamics of instability. Moreover, the hog cycle can be expelled from theory by assuming that pig-breeders predict well, but this assumption does not change the hog market itself. Muth set a regressive development in motion by adapting 'reality' to an outmoded equilibrium theory. His followers made matters even worse by assuming that the individuals had in mind not only the neo-classical model but in addition monetaristic theory, which says that expected changes in the quantity of money exert no influence on real quantities. Thus via rational expectations the world is forced back to the fictions of Walrasian neo-classicism. In this world every form of Keynesian policy is ineffective, because the neo-classical model excludes this effectiveness. That comes about because it is assumed that ordinary people are in fact in agreement with Ratex: they expect that tax reductions are not permanent, that the deficit forces the interest rate up etc. That is then called 'rational': the housewives and the shopkeepers and the crude oil producers and the shipbuilders have brains that reproduce reality, where reality means the abstruse models in the spirit of Walras with a monetary extension. And *therefore* those models form a correct description of reality. And *therefore* the Keynesian description of reality is not correct: the assumed model in people's minds excludes every Keynesian reaction.

This Ratex theory has a certain arrogance about it. Not only do its inventors – these are in particular Robert Lucas et al., who have thus also been joined by the turncoat Keynesian Mark Willis – denounce the Keynesian theory, but in addition please note the theological reasoning with which they do so. The *correct* information about reality is neo-classical, and *therefore* this is in people's minds. Lucas has in advance called *all* rational people to witness. Have the Ratex adherents examined people's faith? Certainly not. They have proved that reality will behave in a neo-classical way if everyone is expected to behave in that way.

And that is, of course, begging the question. For suppose now that all actors are constantly in search of profitable transactions and that suppliers of goods and labour constantly undercut one another, so that the markets for individual goods tend to clear. Does that mean to say that underspending and unemployment are out of the question? Certainly not. The world may even then behave in a highly unstable manner. All those price cuts and wage reductions, all those forms of trial and error, have purchasing power effects that counteract the positive price effects on the volumes. In a period of contraction reductions of the price level do not have a stabilizing effect; they do not stop the shrinkage, even if everyone might believe that they would find work at a lower money wage. Their micro-illusion does not fit in with the structure of incomes and spending, and that is precisely what the Keynesians claim. They assert that people reduce their consumption if their income contracts, and that this reaction passes the shrinkage on. Keynesians further believe that entrepreneurs react to contracting sales by investing less – from a businessman's point of view that is rather rational. The neo-classical school is right only if everyone, and above all the investing entrepreneur, is constantly in an exuberant mood of expansion and optimism – in that case there is no underspending. If one is prepared to describe this example of animal spirits as 'rational', the Ratex school is saved. But we already knew that recessions can disappear by psychological forces.

Willis et al. are of course correct to say that expectations determine people's behaviour and that these expectations can be formulated in many ways – as somewhat dumb adaptations to past experience, or as smart reactions to expected developments. The latter is perhaps more realistic, and it is certain that on that basis interesting models can be developed. We have already known that since the duopoly theory and since the theory of games – we can predict all kinds of results, depending on our hypotheses concerning information and expectations. It is therefore definitely important to investigate what in fact the expectations are of housewives, entrepreneurs, union leaders and investors, and by what models such expectations are best described. I have the feeling that these 'actors' are led by a Gestalt, and we should like to know what exactly that Gestalt looks like – how much *falsches Bewusstsein* plays a part in it, how much smartness and how much stupidity, and what the consequences are of that. The Ratex school makes a contribution to that discussion, but it is a highly specific one, because it assumes in advance that the neo-classical Gestalt gives the correct description of the world and that the actors are aware of this. I don't blame the Ratexists for making highly specific assumptions, but I do for their aggression towards the Keynesians, who in my opinion operate with more common sense. And I also blame them for interpreting unemployment as a voluntary something, as a kind of holiday.

That brings me to the position of the unhyphenated Post Keynesians, a movement congenial to me. I recommend Jan Kregel's *The Reconstruction of Political Economy* (London, 1973). Their story is told in this collection by Paul Davidson. This school is derived from Joan Robinson, Nicholas Kaldor and Piero Sraffa (6); it further goes back to everything that is slightly unorthodox, such as Thorstein Veblen, the institutionalists, John Kenneth Galbraith and a touch of Marx, insofar as usable. Attention is particularly directed towards the obvious characteristics of the modern world, such as the large corporations, the unions, technical development, environmental pollution and the like. It all looks broad and tolerant, and so Paul Davidson calls his essay: *Post Keynesian economics: solving the crisis in economic theory.* Is this trend in fact the new candidate for the new mainstream?

Unfortunately no, not entirely. On one point they are very intolerant, and that concerns neo-classical theory. Everything is allowed, but market equilibrium and marginal productivity (especially that of capital) are *verboten.* Here there is an echo of Joan Robinson's description of the marginal productivity theory as a 'harmful swindle'. There is also something of an echo of the strange preference for rigid coefficients that plays some Keynesians (such as Kaldor) false. Substitution under the influence of price incentives seems to be a bad thing. Davidson too is most vigorous in his condemnation of the neo-classical, neo-Keynesian mainstream. I consider that to be wrong. Not if Davidson means that the Walrasian system fails as a description of reality – nearly everyone, with the exception of Ratex, is of that opinion. Nor if Davidson has something against the neo-classical revival via the Ratex trick. He has my support on these points. But the Post Keynesians go too far when they create the impression that they shake themselves free of the price theory, with its approximate equality of prices and marginal costs, and above all if they reject the neo-classical theory of income distribution. True, this is incomplete – it contains no unions, no modern corporations, profit remains unexplained – but it can be supplemented, improved, made more realistic. James Dean rightly says in the same collection (p. 32): 'there is an Adam Smith in every economist', and the Post Keynesians must not cast out that part of our personality. By doing so they forfeit their candidacy for the new mainstream.

This applies even more strongly to income distribution. What is needed here is obvious: a synthesis between the fundamental truths of the marginal productivity theory and the facts of life of a modern society, such as collective wage bargaining and price determination on a cost-plus basis. The Post Keynesians rightly point to the power of the strong institutions that dominate their environment. Yet nobody can deny that scarcity relations also play a part on the labour market, particularly where wage relations between the compartments are concerned. The latter is the point of departure of fruitful empirical research work by Jan Tinbergen and Joop Hartog (7). This relates to the capacities of workers, to the specifications of the job – real humane economics, in the spirit of the Post Keynesians, but nevertheless also typically neo-classical. As regards the nominal level of all wages and salaries, i.e. the macro approach, the Post Keynesians are right that relative power is decisive. That is why we have constructed spiral models. But then a classical element returns: the real wage level depends not so much on money wages as on productivity, and employment depends on the employers, who are not keen to continue to employ people whose marginal productivity is lower than the wage – all unmistakable neo-classical elements. In addition interest and profit must then be explained; here too we have to call on everything that economics has to offer, including monetary factors. It is true that the neo-classicists are able to tell us little about profit, but that also applies to the Post Keynesians themselves. The whole question of distribution is a peculiar mix of freedom, power and economic determination, and we can get a grip on that mix only if we are prepared to bear power, scarcity and marginal productivity in mind. Tolerance, not denunciation, can help us, and that is something in which the Post Keynesians are deficient when they attack neo-classical theory. That is clear to see from Davidson's essay. He writes in rather bitter terms about the neo-classical school. He says that 'the flavor of some of Keynes' specific policy recommendations was retained, but the essential *logic* of Keynes' economic theory was discarded' (p. 151). This critique is aimed at Samuelson, Solow, Tobin, Hicks. In this sense the Post Keynesians fail to make the connection with the mainstream.

This collection, which I'm briefly describing because it typifies a spectacular but slightly destructive approach, lacks a good essay on the most synthetic trend that exists: the econometrics of the big models. There is nobody to speak for the Tinbergen–Klein–Hickman school. This school seeks the structure of society. This omission is an injustice to the centripetal nature of the mainstream, and fringe phenomena get the upper hand. Perhaps it is characteristic of the compilers' environment that in the fairly incomprehensible concluding essay by Irving Kristol the crucial sentence occurs: 'Keynes' originality lay in taking 'wage stickiness' (the reluctance of the price of labor to fall when unemployment is widespread) as a permanent fact of

modern economy ...' (p. 209). Anyone who is aware of the
fact that Keynes, in the nineteenth chapter of the *General
Theory,* considered the level of money wages unimportant
to employment, so that 'wage stickiness' can hardly be
blamed for anything at all, and in addition anyone who is
of the opinion that wage rigidity is a *classical* cause of unemployment – that anyone must take an odd view of Irving
Kristol's ideas. The man is a sociologist, but occasionally
he associates with economists. What kind of company is it
that he keeps?

This collection gives a misleading picture of a house of
intellect that is engaged in falling to pieces. Admittedly, we
cannot close our eyes to a change that has taken place in
two decades. In 1960 *The End of Ideology* was published,
Daniel Bell's rose-coloured description of a pluralistic economic environment, a combination of the welfare state and
a growing market sector, in which pluralistic opinion-forming prevails, with stimulating debates, but without division
in the world of ideas – and 21 years later the same author
helped with the publication of *The Crisis in Economic
Theory.* If we extrapolate that change, an intellectual explo-
sion follows in the year 2000. Economists will burst like
meteors.

That extrapolation is of course nonsense. The development of the profession tends rather to proceed in waves.
Forces operate that keep opinions together and others that
separate them, and sometimes the latter are stronger. The
logic is neutral, and resembles not only the railways (the
metaphor used above) but also the well-known elastic credit system from cyclical theory: it renders wild cycles possi-

ble. The sharp increase in the number of young professional colleagues who have read Thomas Kuhn (8) has a cen-
trifugal effect; they have understood that occasionally a
revolution has to happen, and that such a revolution means
that old theories and old economists have to be discarded.
Hence Lucas' repeated insistence on the advanced age of
the Keynesians, something which, apart from the viewpoint of good taste, there would be no objection to if the
complainant could produce something better than his improbable story about rational expectations.

What is new and fashionable has a stimulating effect.
Economists are no different from other thinking beings to
the extent that they are stimulated by the announcement of
entirely fresh insights. A vigorous incentive is to be found
there for the conceivers of potential novelties. The disadvantage is obvious: economics is carried along by fashionable waves, and the idea gains ground that the whole profession, as from today, will be turned upside down. That
must not happen. The waves have to break in 'normal
science'. Keynesianism was such a wave, as was monetarism and the supply-side philosophy. Alternative views, intended to undermine conventional wisdom, can be taken
along: the sheepskin theory of education, the bureaucratic
theory of salary differences, the feminist theory of discrimination. All that can be absorbed by the *corpus* of economics. Undue attention to the novel and the momentaneous
should be rebutted. Again and again someone must appear
who answers the King's question about what is new in
*Wissenschaft* by the Kantian reply: *Majestaet kennen schon
das Alte?* For innovation is a fine thing as long as the old

grows in volume and acceptance. Yet parts of the old views must be banished.

This brings me to the delicate question that has been constantly present in my mind when writing this essay: what, in the debate among economists, is the optimum balance between tolerance and aggressiveness? I should prefer to subscribe to Tinbergen's admonition when he said in 1983: 'economists must stop with their confrontations'. 'They must aim at a synthesis' (9). He said that with a view to the urgent practical problems – unemployment, stagnation, the crisis of the welfare state, the threatening environmental disasters. I dare say, but the above has made it clear that there are exceptions to this rule. There are cases in which the differences of opinion have to be exposed to the light of day and not papered over. A synthesis is sometimes possible, sometimes not. Sometimes tolerance is counterproductive.

In the first place, on deductive grounds, inconsistency must be rejected. Logic is logic and false logic is false logic. We saw that at least three issues, and probably more, are still undecided on purely logical grounds.

In the second place, on empirical grounds, the improbable must be rejected. After all, we have for this the Neyman-Pearson rules for statistical inference (10), which ensure that we are not too tolerant, and leave false hypotheses standing, but again not too intolerant, so that we reject possibly correct hypotheses. Nothwithstanding the formal clarity of these rules, the debates on implicit or explicit parameters are uncertain and widespread.

In the third place, we must signal selective observation,

which in itself does not imply a fallacy, but does give rise
to a debate on relevance – and that is a moral debate. A
certain indignation cannot be excluded from such a debate,
and the most that we can insist on is that rhetoric is kept
fairly decent.

In the fourth place, we are concerned in economics with
colligation, like it or not, and occasionally there will have
to be conflicts in this field. But we could try to make a distinction between stories which, though they differ, do not
do so to an unacceptable extent, and genuine overdetermination, in which the stories are contradictory. It would
be a welcome contribution to the economic discourse if
these two cases were kept separate, for only in the latter
case is dispute inevitable.

In the fifth place, differences of opinion will always continue to exist about policy advice. Tolerance finds its natural limits in the fact that governments cannot do everything
at the same time. Still, here we must follow Tinbergen's
lead, which entails that targets and instruments must be differentiated as closely as possible. That yields many complications, but nevertheless we have to keep on trying it.

The real moral dilemmas come about when we have to
react to intolerance (for instance that of the rational expectations school and of some Post Keynesians), to insensitivi-
ty (unemployment is a holiday) and to incitement to mental
or physical violence (the Marxists). These are reprehensible
or even evil things that have to be unmasked, above all
when they present themselves in the form of metaphors.
That is why Marxism has to be rejected hook, line and
sinker. It is an old paradox: how tolerant must we be to-

wards the intolerant? It is not only democracy that is confronted with this paradox, but also the invisible college of
scientists. Unfortunately, a ready-made solution is not to
hand. But there is no reason for despair.

For the mainstream of economics is in fairly good shape.
Certainly, it is not crystal clear. All kinds of things are carried along by it – unsolved problems, and debris. We see
whirlpools of intellectual confusion. But the water is safe
to drink and the river is flowing in the right direction.

(1)It has seldom been attempted to probe the consensus empirically. A
praiseworthy exception is the research by Bruno S. Frey, Victor Ginsburgh, Pierre Pestieau, Werner W. Pommerehne and Friedrich Schneider:
Consensus, Dissension and Ideology among Economists in Various European Countries and the United States, *European Economic Review*, Vol.
23, 1983, p. 59. They submitted twenty-two statements of both an analytical and a normative nature to a large number of colleagues (fiscal policy
has a stimulating impact, income distribution should be more equal etc.).
The colleagues were asked to agree, to agree with reservations or to reject
the statements; it characterizes the profession that roughly a third
opted for the middle choice. The authors conclude 'that there exists a considerable amount of consensus among economists, but that there are also
substantial differences between countries and ideological views'. And also:
'the differences are, as expected, particularly strong on those propositions
which are normatively phrased or which have a clear ideological content'.
The latter applies above all to France. The authors raise the question
whether these disagreements are greater or smaller than among non-economists, but cannot of course answer this question, because the non-economists have not been investigated. We hope, of course, that economists
will display a smaller spread. I consider this investigation most useful as
a start, but, as we have seen above, it has not yielded a basis for interesting
conclusions. It deserves to be emulated, but then concentrated on more
specific questions, with the theoretical and the normative being kept separate. Precisely among economists it is possible to ask sharp questions, for
instance about the value of elasticities that someone has in mind.
(2)The question is whether the analysis of human motivation in fact includes all the mainsprings. See for instance the remarkable book: *The New*

*World of Economics* (Homewood, 1975) by Richard B. McKenzie and Gordon Tullock, followers of Gary Becker. They describe the mental processes of actors who are on the point of marrying, burgling, reproducing themselves, lying etc. The decisions are interpreted as the result of a cost–benefit analysis. In itself there is nothing against this, provided that the analysing economist makes allowance for the moral values and the group norms of the decision-maker. Violation of such standards entails psychical costs; many actors are troubled more by their conscience than by external stimuli, and among the external stimuli approval or rejection by the group plays a part, though we don't know exactly what. Now McKenzie and Tullock try to distance themselves precisely from these moral and sociological motives. Their reasoning leads us to strange ideas. The authors point out for instance that the behaviour of individuals in a riot has to be explained not so much by a *psychologie des foules* as by a limited risk of being caught. Someone can steal with impunity while the stones are flying through the air. But the authors take care not to consider how riots come about. If we follow their theory we could reason as follows: riots are invoked all the more easily if individuals have time on their hands and low incomes from other forms of activity. Those are conditions that are met in a situation of high unemployment. We may therefore expect lots of riots and little chance of the offenders being caught. But this sombre forecast holds good only if we ignore the moral factor. The group norms are relevant. That applies above all in the welfare state, and even more so if the welfare state is in a crisis. Anyone desirous of getting to know the norms must study them. They can have a positive effect (increased solidarity, and the feeling that unemployment can affect me as well). But a negative one too: some Marxists are in favour of 'proletarian shopping' (i.e. shoplifting) as a manifestation of the class struggle. If that Gestalt spreads, together with unemployment, interesting times await us. The repeated crash of glass. Anyone who denies that norms play a part in processes as described by McKenzie and Tullock does economics a particular disservice. There is a point here that micro-economists do not discuss sufficiently.

(3) This refers to John Muellbauer and Richard Portes' chapter in William H. Branson, *Macroeconomic Theory and Policy*, New York etc., 1979 – the best textbook on the subject I ever came across – but the 'Keynesian' case in the Muellbauer–Portes chapter is not recognizable to a Keynesian like me. It is characterized by a nominal wage level which is too high with respect to the price level. If this is a quantity-constrained disequilibrium, it looks like a classical one, with a stock of money that is too small.

(4)The polarizing authors of *Why Economists Disagree,* that book with an unpleasant smell to it. See Chapter I, footnote 5.

(5)J.F. Muth, Rational Expectations and the Theory of Price Movements, *Econometrica,* July, 1961, p. 315.

(6)Piero Sraffa is one of the most peculiar cases among economists. You could compile a sociology of the subcultures of economists by asking them how they react to his name. Most of my colleagues (another of my hypotheses) have heard of this eminent scholar, but hardly anyone can explain what he has discovered, except perhaps that he demonstrated in 1926 that firms often pursue a higher price than corresponds to full utilization, and that he published Ricardo's work. But there is a tremendous literature on Sraffa. Why? What is in fact the contribution of that strange book with that strange title (*Production of Commodities By Means of Commodities,* Cambridge, 1960)? Sraffa thought for fifty years before he produced these ninety-nine pages, and some circles come pretty close to worshipping him. Why? Surely not because he invented the *Standard Commodity?* The Standard Commodity does not change in value if income distribution changes, so that the neo-Ricardians have one worry less (though they have problems enough left). Surely not for proving that relative prices and the price level are two different things? Surely not for having written an intellectually satisfying, refined tract – crystal-clear but hardly relevant – showing for instance that the different productive inputs can be 'reduced to dated quantities of labour'? There is nothing in these exercises that appeals to the Post Keynesian desire for a humane type of economics, close to the throbbing heart of the people. It is also somewhat surprising that the special issue of *Social Research* (1983), devoted to the Great Thinkers of Today, which contains essays on Foucault, Marcuse, Habermas, Wittgenstein and Popper, also contains a piece on Sraffa. It is written by P.R. Wolff. Highly recommended to anyone who wants to see the riddle of Sraffa's popularity among Post Keynesians solved and who can't make head or tail of *Production of Commodities By Means of Commodities.*

(7)Jan Tinbergen, *Income Distribution, Analysis and Policies,* Amsterdam, Oxford, New York, 1975. This is a supply and demand theory, with elements of the human capital school and marginal productivity. The wage structure is broadly explained. Moreover, Tinbergen takes into account the possibility that people do not completely meet the requirements that their job makes of them. The latter idea has been elaborated by Joop Hartog, *Income Distribution, A Multicapability Theory,* Boston, The Hague and London, 1982. Hartog goes much further than Tinbergen to the extent that he investigates a large number of job specifications described in collective labour agreements.

(8)*The Structure of Scientific Revolutions*, Chicago, 1970 (2nd edition).
(9)Jan Tinbergen, De noodzaak van een synthese, *ESB*, 1982, p. 1284.
(10)Mark Blaug, *The Methodology of Economics or How Economists Explain*, Cambridge, 1980, p. 20.

Chapter XIV

# A MORAL FOR ECONOMISTS

Are economists indispensable? If the profession did not exist, people would be freer in their views. Everyone would
be his or her own economist, which is also the case now,
but the wheel and Adam Smith would have to be reinvent-
ed again and again. That is hardly efficient. Politicians
would be less constrained in their colligative efforts. Democracy would suffer from a lack of knowledge among the citizens. The danger of hearsay, wild rumours, false general-
ization from micro-experience, would have a clear field. Let
us assume that the profession is indeed indispensable.

But that makes requirements. Economics is a serious
subject. This is occasionally forgotten by the academic subculture. One of the temptations of logic and high theory is
that we treat the whole business frivolously. It's one big
game, all those models and systems, all those novelties, all
those intellectual tournaments, all those conferences in
agreeable summer resorts, all those journals providing out-
lets for schools and departments, all those new books sug-
gesting quite new insights (for instance the insight that economic statements can be classified in seven categories and
that this typology makes sense when we discuss the culture
of economics). The whole game easily breeds a kind of elat-

ed scepticism. Economics is not only a living, it's a great
pastime as well.

This frivolous approach detracts from one of the duties
of the academic economist: to contribute to the mainstream, to reduce folly in the public discourse and, if possible, to rationalize economic policy. That requires a synthesis, eclecticism and the right degree of tolerance. These
objectives are harmed if too many economists devote their
energy to finding elegant solutions to barely relevant problems and forget to establish a link with the other economic
subcultures, notably that of the storytellers, the journalists
and the politicians. I do not recommend that all economists
concentrate on empirical work, and even less that they try
to vulgarize their research findings. But I should like the
majority to keep an eye on the needs of the citizens. Relevance may not be displaced by elegance, at least not on a
large scale. The call for theoretical revolutions – the new
Marx! the new Keynes! – may not undermine the mainstream.
And economic theorists should try to communicate.

The last recommendation applies above all to the econometric subculture. Communication with the rest of the
economists, and if possible with laymen too, is essential to
the progress of the discipline. Whether economics has a future, and whether disagreements are to be solved in an or-
derly manner, depends on the cooperation between econometricians and general economists. At present this cooperation leaves something to be desired. The most embarras-
sing gaps in our knowledge are caused by ignorance of the
strategic parameters that are implied in our views and our
stories. The most striking example concerns the unsolved

question whether budgetary deficits are good or bad for recovery, but it also relates to the dispute between neo-classical and Post Keynesian observers. 'It's all a matter of elasticities' – well, that seems an easy sledge-hammer argu
ment, but it does contain some truth. A crystal-clear insight
into these parameters is perhaps beyond the capabilities of
the human mind, but economists should not give up on it.

The subculture of the storytellers and the politicians is
not exposed to the temptation of irrelevance and frivolity.
On the contrary, these are serious people – their numbers
include fanatics. They also have a sufficient tendency towards communication. My admonitions to them are different. They relate to their tendency to tell tall tales, in which
strong value judgments (and sometimes hatred) overrule
common sense; they use false images and metaphors; they
jump from *is* to *ought;* they lean heavily on verification and
eliminate undesired information. Stories should be good
stories, coherent, realistic, morally beyond reproach and, if
possible, elevating. And in any case this subculture should
make use of the results of empirical science. If falsifiable
truth is anchored anywhere, it is there.

But the latter of course requires that the communication
comes from two sides. Economic scientists may demand
that their results are taken into account, but then only if
they are prepared to present these results in an understandable way. They must take the problems of the citizens and
the politicians seriously, and talk to them. They must also
listen. One of the psychological laws of communication is
that the process succeeds only if the participants show no
signs of contempt, scorn and disdain. Only in that way can

differences of opinion be bridged and economists make themselves indispensable.

I am writing down these moral recommendations with a certain reluctance – preaching is rather distasteful, especially if the preacher does not always practise what he preaches – but there is justification to be found in the prisoner's dilemma. Every school and every individual economist has a partial and short-sighted interest in a strategy in which debates are over-accentuated and disagreements are inflamed. Sarcasm leads to rhetorical success. No institutional arrangement exists for damping these processes. In the corporate subculture things are different – there economic experts are forced to cooperate with one another and with engineers, legal specialists, accountants, public relations people. There communication, synthesis and eclecticism are imposed by the organization. The overall result is improved by this. Perhaps economists could take an example from this subculture by observing some self-control. Differences of opinion could as a result be more easily localized, relativized and bridged.

These admonitions are supported by the economic tasks of the present day. If we lived in quiet times, with Walrasian characteristics, frivolity would meet with little objection. Intellectual conflicts would contribute only to the liveliness; creativity would be permitted to lead to nonsense. We could manage without economists. Economic policy would barely be required; the clock runs by itself. Unfortunately, tranquillity is not a feature of the contemporary economic scene. Unemployment is alarming. The welfare state is crumbling. The environment is under threat. The international financial system is tottering. Developing countries are being restrained in their development. In those threatening circumstances economists should strengthen their cooperation, their communication and their personality. They are faced with the task of arriving at concerted results while retaining their own political objectives, their own views and their own identity. Cooperation is good for the profession. Let us hope that what is good for economists is good for society.

# INDEX OF NAMES

* Arjo Klamer is not mentioned in this book. His exciting 'The New
Classical Macroeconomics, Conversations with New Classical Economists and their Opponents' (Brighton, 1984) came to my attention when
the text of 'Among Economists' was completed. Klamer's talks with Lucas, Sargent, Tobin, Solow, Blinder c.s. demonstrate that there exists a
rhetoric of economics which uses arguments not often found in research
papers. The book is very revealing. The critics do not spare Ratex: 'I find
that fundamental framework ludicrous' says Robert Solow. And Alan
Blinder on market clearing: 'Somehow, some people are able to look at
the world and not see involuntary unemployment. I think I see it all over
the place during cyclical downturns.' Even more revealing are the statements of the certified members of Ratex. Thomas J. Sargent on the thirties: 'I do not have a theory, nor do I know somebody else's theory that
constitutes a satisfactory explanation of the Great Depression.' Robert
Lucas: 'If you look back at the 1929 to 1933 episode, there were a lot of
decisions made that, after the fact, people wished they had never made;
there were a lot of jobs people quit that they wished they had hung on
to; there were a lot of job offers that people turned down because they
thought the wage offer was too crappy.' The reader wonders whether Lucas and Sargent indeed use all the information available – one gets the
impression that they do not recognize a depression if they meet it in the
street. The same question arises when Lucas says to Klamer: 'Everybody
likes the idea of rational expectations. It is hardly controversial.' Really?